for Adrian
   I do hope you find this interesting – it was written from the heart.

A SPECIAL
A DUTY

Sincere good wishes

Jennifer Etkin

by

JENNIFER E·····

GW00536434

**Grosvenor House
Publishing Limited**

This book is published by
Grosvenor House Publishing Ltd
28-30 High Street, Guildford, Surrey, GU1 3EL.
www.grosvenorhousepublishing.co.uk

A CIP record for this book
is available from the British Library

ISBN 978-1-78148-697-9

Cover design by Jennifer Elkin
with background image courtesy of Siiri Kumari

For
Rita, Pat and Susan
'The Team'

*With someone like you, a pal so
good and true...*

Rita, Pat, Susan and Jennifer (The Team), Ludlow 1951

CONTENTS

THE CREW

The Halifax bomber flew with a crew of seven and, although duty personnel stepped in from time to time to fill a crew position due to illness or leave requirement, the following airmen formed the Storey crew for the six month period of operational flying with 148 Squadron:

1943/44

Position	Nov	Dec	Jan	Feb	Mar	Apr
	First Operational Tour (45 sorties)			Second Operational Tour (6 sorties)		
Pilot	T. Storey..					
Bomb Aimer	P.Crosland...T.R.Lawman............E.Elkington-Smith..........................					
Navigator	W.W. Nichol..................O.W.Congdon..					
Wireless Operator	W.G. Davis...					
Flight Engineer	C.J. Keen..					
Air Gunner	J.C.Hughes...					
Despatcher	G. Fidler..P. Stradling....................					

FOREWORD

There was a widespread and popular belief, at the start of World War II, that to be a pilot, a man had to be tall, blond, blue eyed, very handsome and required to wear at all times a white silk scarf wound loosely round the neck with one end free to catch the wind. Seriously though, with the rapid expansion of Air Forces at the outbreak of World War II, the attributes for those who opted for flying training were thankfully less idyllic and more relevant to the urgency that existed. This allowed me to get a foot in. All 'would be' aviators had to volunteer first, then pass stringent health checks, a maths exam, and have a minimum length of leg. You may well ask! It was to reach the rudder pedals in some aircraft.

Flying training required the pupil to attain proficiency in placing the aircraft in every possible configuration of aerobatic manoeuvre with the utmost accuracy and safety, whilst obeying every air regulation in the book. This included a total ban on low flying, a most dangerous and often fatal practice. As a fully trained pilot, Tom Storey, flying a four-engine Halifax aircraft, was assigned to an RAF squadron engaged in secret Special Duties. This type of operation required him to deliberately ignore the low flying safety regulation, descending to very low altitudes in hilly or mountainous terrain, deep into enemy-held territory. These clandestine operations of between seven and ten hours' duration, under cover of darkness, required the skills of flying and accurate navigation to determine success or failure.

Tom captained the crew of seven, a lone, independent unit of very young men who had to grow up fast.

Larry Toft
World War II Special Duty Halifax Pilot

INTRODUCTION

This is an account of a young RAF pilot, Tom Storey, during six months of operational flying with 148 Special Duty Squadron in the Mediterranean, the Balkans and Poland during World War II, and an attempt to understand the reasons for his death twenty years later. These aircrews were brave and skilful beyond their years and my admiration for them has grown throughout the progress of this work. This story is personal because Tom Storey was my father, but many families had their lives unravelled by the trauma that war leaves in its wake; it is a story as relevant today as it was seventy years ago.

One of the reasons I wanted to write a story about my father's time with 148 Squadron was that first, I have acquired quite a lot of information over the years and it seemed wrong just to sit on that and do nothing with it and, secondly, it is a personal journey for me, an attempt to lay some ghosts to rest. My father never talked about his wartime experiences, maybe because of the inherent secrecy of the work, or maybe because he could not bear to recall that time, so I have little first-hand information other than a discussion with Charlie Keen, flight engineer on my father's crew, and written accounts by other crew members; bomb aimer, Eddie Elkington-Smith and wireless operator, Walter Davis. I met Walter Davis in 2013 and he and his daughter, Anne Black, not only shared photographs and letters with me, but gave me access to his flying logbook, which contained a record of all the flights, more than forty, that he had made with Tom. Paul Lashmar, journalist and documentary maker, generously shared the research material he had gathered about my father's last flight, and Mike Bedford-Stradling, son of crewmember Patrick Stradling, kindly provided me with material from his father's archive. It is the personal nature of this story which I hope will convey adequately the magnificence of ordinary men in extraordinary circumstances.

I have tried to present, as accurately as possible, the context in which my father and his crew were operating, and the conditions in which they lived. I believe the truth is in the facts. I have used a combination of Squadron operational records, personal accounts, and information gleaned from an excellent selection of books written on the subject. I hope I do those authors justice in my own account, and, more importantly, honour those profoundly brave young men, who operated in secrecy and, until very recently, with little in the way of recognition or memorials.

THURSDAY 23rd APRIL 1964

I remember running very fast downhill to the telephone box. Running so fast that my heart nearly pounded out of my chest, but I couldn't slow down, I had to go faster still. I was 16 and had come home from school on the bus with my sister Susan. We dropped our schoolbags on the kitchen floor and ran upstairs to say hello to Dad. He had been in bed for a couple of days – it being the anniversary. The anniversary meant getting very drunk most years, but this year he was out of work and there was no money for drinking. He had found oblivion in a bottle of sleeping tablets and we skipped into the room to find him dead, lying in bed with the covers pulled up and one arm hanging over the side. Lots of shouting, Mum rushing upstairs, an untouched cup of tea on the floor by the bed, "Get an ambulance, quick". I could barely find breath to get the words out. "Come quickly, I think he's dead." The sirens reached the house before I did. Resuscitation failed, doctor serious and resigned, hope falling away and desperation filling the room, he was gone. The coroner decided the balance of his mind had been disturbed, and he was right to think that, but not right to say that he took his own life. He simply couldn't face that day, the 23rd April, and needed to blot it out – his inner turmoil reached an unbearable pitch on that day every year.

I can't say what caused such pain because he didn't talk about it, and even if he could tell us what he had done during that winter and spring of 1943/44, perhaps the pain was from what he failed to do, or what he felt he should have done, rather than anything he actually did. Maybe the pain was because those events of 1944 were a high point of madness and thrilling adventure, never to be recaptured in the peacetime world of work and family. Did working as a commercial traveller for a soft drinks company suck the remaining life out of the returning hero? Or did he feel he was lucky to have any job, and berated himself for having thrown it all away because of the memories. For twenty years he had been troubled, and we had grown quite used to it. Life in our home always carried on with as much normality as possible thanks to the strength and resourcefulness of Rita, my mother. She didn't understand either, but loved her husband enough to take up the cup of tea that lay cold at the bedside, when she could have said: "For goodness sake get up and stop feeling sorry for yourself". Doctor Brown, in his struggle to find comforting words for us said that it was: "Maybe for the best", and, although he meant well, he was quite wrong. It was not for the best at all. The despair didn't die with him – we had breathed in too much of it to ever be fully free ourselves. Yet we survived – our little team of Rita, Pat, Jennifer and Susan.

I can never know what lay behind such strong feelings about the 23rd April, but it was a day that held terrors to be escaped from in any way possible. I would like to understand, but I may just have to tell the story of those months – the winter and spring 1943-44 – and accept that sometimes a person's experiences are so unique and personal, that not even a loving daughter can unravel the threads.

CHAPTER 1

ARRIVAL AT TOCRA

F/Sgt Tom Storey 1943

Tom Storey left Bournemouth's Hurn airport on the 23th October 1943, bound for Tocra on the Cyrenaican coast of Libya, with a fresh, young crew, a modified Handley Page Halifax Bomber and little idea of what he had volunteered for. He had returned from pilot training in Canada to complete the final stage of training for four-engine heavy bombers in the United Kingdom and was expecting to be posted to one of the bomber squadrons, when a briefing officer came looking for two volunteer crews with good navigational skills for overseas work. Tom's navigator was a commissioned RCAF[1] officer, who had been an instructor in his native Canada, and Walter Davis, the wireless operator, felt that this made them ideal for the assignment and enthusiastically persuaded Tom, the pilot, to sign them up. Walter always said he coerced Tom into volunteering, but I suspect it was an attractive proposition to them all, particularly as the life-expectancy for bomber crews was four missions. Maybe the 'unknown' was more attractive than the 'known'. They were accepted for the work and went

---

[1] Royal Canadian Air Force.

to RAF Lyneham in Wiltshire for further training, to collect their aircraft, and to receive instructions for joining their new Squadron, which was based in North Africa. They still had little idea of what they had volunteered for, but there were clues when, on the 2nd October, 1943 they collected their aircraft, a Handley Page, Mark II Halifax (number JN888), which appeared to have some strange modifications. The mid upper turret had been removed; there was no nose armament and a huge hole had been cut into the floor with opening doors. This, they suspected, pointed to supply work, but the briefing officer had told them: "I can say no more". So they didn't ask.

They carried out a series of wireless, electrical and fuel-consumption tests before taking off for their departure point, Hurn airport, but were barely twenty minutes into the flight when engine failure forced them to turn back. They made it at the next attempt, and ten days later received their final briefing for the flight to North Africa, during which they were warned to keep a sharp lookout for fighter planes over the Bay of Biscay, which was known to be a training area for new German pilots. Taking off at the same time was a Wellington Bomber, piloted by one of Tom's friends, and there was a bit of nervous banter between the crews as to who would get there first before they took off on the nine-hour flight to Rabat, in Morocco. All went smoothly for the Storey crew, but the Wellington did not arrive and they were unable to find out what had happened to the crew.[2] Mercifully they had little time to dwell on this before taking off for the second stage of the trip, which was to Castel Benito in Tripoli and then on to their final destination of Tocra, in Libya.

At Tocra they were met by Wing Commander James Blackburn, who, they noticed, wore no mark of rank or medals, and a

---

[2] Hurn records show Wellington HZ895 taking off for Rabat Sale 30 minutes after the Storey crew, but landing at Chivenor with engine trouble. It returned to Hurn for re-despatch.

Squadron Leader, both of whom were keen to examine the aircraft, which was a new Mark of the Halifax model. The modifications, as the crew had suspected, did indeed mean supply work, and it was explained to them that the Squadron, which came under Mediterranean Command, was involved in supplying and infiltrating personnel to the growing resistance movements in Greece and the Balkans. The aircraft of the Squadron, like their own, had been modified for supply work; the only armament being four Browning machine guns mounted in the rear turret. They flew alone at night and without fighter escort to remote locations with only fires and hand-held torches to guide them in when they arrived. The requirement for a good navigator became clear, as did the need for a skilled pilot. The winter of 1943/44 would prove to have the worst weather over Europe and the Balkans in twenty years and, with many of the dropping grounds in deep valleys, the pilot needed to be able to handle the aircraft in conditions close to its operational limit. Tom Storey, twenty-three years of age, had learned to fly in Canada, converting to heavy bombers back in England; his flying ability and nerve would be tested to the limit in the coming months. He had joined a group of elite crews flying missions that made no headlines at the time and, with the exception of a handful of memorials scattered through the Balkans and Poland, have received little recognition since.

Conditions at Tocra base must have come as a shock. The Squadron had recently moved there from Derna and the ops room was just a tent on the south side of the runway, with the crews billeted in a further scattering of tents around the perimeter. On arrival the navigator, being an officer, cycled off to the officers' mess on the bicycle he had brought with him on the aircraft, while the rest of the crew, being non-commissioned officers, were given a tent and told to dig a trench around it (to cope with the heavy rains when they came). As they unpacked their belongings it became clear that they would have to get used to living with sand, particularly when the desert wind blew, as the red dust got into everything – eyes, hair, clothes and even food, but a lively sense of humour prevailed at the camp and, with the natural resilience of young men, they were soon making the most of a variety of activities such as football, whist drives and gramophone recitals. They had a mobile cinema with regular screenings and each canteen had a darts board to help pass the long hours between sorties and keep the homesickness at bay on this desolate stretch of desert far from home. Three years of fighting in the North-African desert had seen Italian, German and Allied forces chase each other back and forth across this hostile land but it was now firmly in the hands of the Allies. Italy had surrendered in September 1943, and although the tide of war was moving in favour of the Allies it was still necessary to tie up German divisions with the help of resistance groups in the Mediterranean and the Balkans, in order to relieve pressure on Stalin's Eastern Front and divert attention from Allied plans to land in France (Operation Overlord).

Tom's arrival on the North-African coast coincided with a general stand down of operations because of the bad weather, but on the 2nd November, he and his bomb aimer Peter Crosland were given the opportunity to join Flight Lieutenant Brotherton-Ratcliffe, affectionately known as Brother Rat, on a six-hour sortie to Greece. This was their only opportunity to observe an experienced crew in action before beginning their own tour of duty, and it was probably just as well they didn't have long to think about it as the heavy and intense flak encountered during that initial flight must have given them pause for thought. Having returned to base at 0600 from that flight, they were considered ready for ops and took to the skies at dusk with their own crew of Storey, Crosland, Nichol, Davis, Keen, Hughes and Fidler. They were bound for Macedonia and a supply drop to MONKEYWRENCH, one of two very secret Missions that had dropped into the mountainous area of eastern Albania the previous month; the other one being MULLIGATAWNY. These two Missions initially shared drop zones and wireless communications as they made their way into Macedonia to rendezvous with Tito's General 'Tempo'[3], though their Missions would eventually go their separate ways. MULLIGATAWNY, headed by Major Mostyn Davies, would head for the Bulgarian border and attempt to contact and organise factions of the Bulgarian resistance, whereas MONKEYWRENCH would remain in Macedonia, carrying out sabotage operations on vital installations, such as the chrome mines at Skopje. The following cipher from Special Operations Executive HQ in Cairo reveals the nature of the sabotage raids and the subsequent pressure on the Squadron to deliver explosives and equipment to Mission staff and their partisans on the ground:

> "London most anxious cut off German supplies chrome RPT chrome. Send soonest details position Allatine mines. Can you initiate attacks against mine power houses or trains carrying ore? If so what stores required."[i]

Followed by:

> "Most urgent put SKOPLE-VELE-DJEVDJELIJA line out of action. Treat as first priority target. What is earliest date you can attack? Say whether you need sapper assistance."[ii]

Ammunition and explosives were requested by MONKEY-WRENCH for partisan sabotage activities, but Mission staff also asked for personal items such as pipes, tinned soup, water bottles, boots, novels and boiled sweets.[iii] Supply drops were their lifeline but on this particular November night, though they could hear the drone of the Halifax and had lit their fires, the crew in the aircraft above could see nothing. Navigator

---

[3] General Svetozar Vukmanovic.

'Nik' Nichol believed they had passed over the target a couple of times but visibility was too poor to spot anything, so they circled for almost an hour looking for a break in the clouds before fuel began to run low and the task was abandoned. They returned to base, where the concern that night was not the success or failure of supply drops, but the fate of the popular and highly respected Passmore crew, who had taken off for Yugoslavia in Liberator AL509, and failed to return. It was a great loss for the Squadron, who continued to send wireless transmissions to the crew in the vain hope that they would respond. They could not – Flight Lieutenant Maurice Passmore, aged 23, and his entire crew had perished on a mountainside on their way to drop supplies to the FUNGUS Mission in Croatia. When news of the crash reached FUNGUS headquarters, Majors Hunter and Reed made their way to the scene where, with the help of their partisans, they buried the dead, marking the grave in a nearby cemetery with a simple cross bearing their names. It was particularly poignant for Reed because it was the Passmore crew who had dropped his Mission[4] into Croatia three weeks earlier and taken such trouble to ensure that his party went out over the correct location, circling down and down through the mist until, through a gap in the clouds, the lights of the signal fires were spotted.[iv] The loss of this fine crew was mourned by all who knew them and they were later reinterred in the Belgrade War Cemetery.

The following night the Storey crew were the first of three crews to take off for Macedonia and another attempt to drop supplies to MONKEYWRENCH. Weather conditions were poor throughout the flight and cloud obscured the drop zone, giving them little hope of success. Then, unexpectedly, they spotted the fires through a break in the cloud and, after an

---

[4] JUDGE.

exchange of the correct recognition phrases[5] and several dummy runs, they dropped fifteen containers, fourteen packages and twenty-three kitbags, amongst which were flares for a Very pistol.[6] Flight Sergeant Brown in the following Halifax had been forced back by poor weather but Brotherton-Ratcliffe, with supplies for MULLIGATAWNY at the same target, was guided in by the pistol flares which had just been dropped by the Storey crew. This prompted a congratulatory message from the receiving party: "Congratulate pilot MULLIGATAWNY 5 - we directed him in with Very lights from plane load before him." The bad weather that night had forced four of the Squadron Halifaxes back to base and damaged the only remaining Liberator, but there were no casualties and the Storey crew recorded their first successful operation with 148 Squadron.

Having flown three consecutive nights, the crew had a couple of days off, no doubt making good use of the hot showers which had just been set up in the courtyard of Tocra Fort, the new headquarters, made fit for purpose by the hard-working Royal Engineers. The men were issued with half a bar of soap each month for washing themselves and their clothes, so a certain amount of frugality was still needed, but the shower facility was a big improvement. They were also issued with personal first-aid packs by the medical officer, who worked tirelessly to get conditions improved for them. Then, on the 12th November, after a brief period of respite, the crew took off for a special delivery of personnel and supplies to the SPILLWAY Mission of Brigadier 'Trotsky' Davies in Albania. Sitting on the floor of the aircraft were five of the eight-man team, who were to be dropped that night, including Lieutenant

---

[5] AIR 'the flowers that bloom in the spring', GROUND 'have nothing to do with the case'.

[6] A coloured flare fired from a special pistol (Very pistol) for signalling at night.

Jack Dumoulin, a newly-qualified doctor, whose medical stores were packed and ready for despatch with him in the fuselage, and Captain Marcus Lyon, an intelligence officer hand-picked for the mission by Davies himself. The rest of the party, led by Colonel Norman Wheeler, and split between the Storey and Fairweather aircraft, comprised two wireless operators, a paramilitary expert, a Corporal of Horse[7] and Major Gordon Layzell, who would die in a horrible accident within weeks of the drop. A sandstorm had blown up during the afternoon but four crews, including Storeys, got away before Wing Commander Blackburn judged conditions to be too dangerous and suspended operations. During take-off, Tom Storey's Halifax JN888 burst a tyre, as a result of debris on the runway, which also damaged the starboard inner propeller and the fuselage, but with the aircraft full of high octane fuel, he decided to press on with the flight. As they crossed the Greek coastline, there was a loud bang as flak hit the aircraft, but again they carried on and got as far as the Albanian border before severe icing finally forced them to abandon the operation. During the return journey, the crew briefed the passengers that, because of the damage to the wheel they may have to jump out, and it was then up to the pilot to balance the risk factors, bearing in mind that parachutes did occasionally fail to open and, if weather conditions and topography were favourable, it might be safer to land the aircraft with everyone on board. Things were further complicated by the crash landing of a Halifax belonging to 463 Squadron at Tocra, which was obstructing the runway and all returning planes were being diverted to Benina, an airstrip near Benghazi.

Tom made the decision to land the aircraft, and received instructions to jettison the entire load, except for a green container, which he did. There was a lot at stake, with twelve

---

[7] A rank in the British Army's Household Cavalry.

lives resting on his ability to put the aircraft down safely, and this may have prompted his attempt to puncture the good tyre by hanging out through the drop hatch into a 160 mph slipstream and shooting at it with his revolver. The attempt failed. He climbed back into the cockpit and, with all the skill and calm concentration he could muster, brought the aircraft in on a long, low approach over the treeless desert and managed to make a successful three-engine, one-wheel landing[v] with minimal damage and no casualties. Jack Dumoulin, the young medical officer on board that night, commented that crash landing in Libya with one engine out and a large hole in the fuselage was "not a lot of fun"![vi] A landing such as this could never be rehearsed in training; the decisions Tom took that night and the skilful way he handled the aircraft earned him well-deserved praise.[vii] Dumoulin and his shaken colleagues made another attempt to drop to Brigadier Davies's SPILLWAY Mission in mid-November, 1943, but weather conditions were so atrocious that it was decided to drop them into southern Albania and hope that they could eventually link up with Brigadier Davies in the North. They were successfully dropped in during December,[8] but the plan to move north was thwarted by the SPILLWAY Mission Station being attacked and overrun by the Germans a few weeks later.[viii]

Following the crash landing, Tom's trusty Halifax JN888 was patched up by the efficient ground crew and quickly back in service taking Captain Bill Felton, a Royal Army Medical Corps doctor, and Private Goodyer to the Triklinos dropping ground in central Greece. The country was seeing an upsurge in resistance at the end of 1943, following the withdrawal of Italian forces, but as the Germans moved in and took over, they launched ruthless attacks against the guerrilla bands. Added to that, the various factions of the resistance movement were at

---

[8] They were dropped to the SWIFTER Mission, headed by Lt.Col. Alan Palmer

odds with each other and long-standing hostilities had finally broken into full civil war. Mission staff were constantly on the move to keep ahead of the Germans and to avoid the factional fighting breaking out around them. It was into this cauldron that Halifax JN888 prepared to drop Felton and Goodyer. Tom was concerned that the target, over Triklinos, didn't match the one given at the briefing, but the three signal fires were correctly placed and the letter 'G' flashed from the aircraft was answered correctly. After circling for some time the men jumped out from three-thousand feet and their parachutes were seen to open safely. The first patient for Captain Felton was Captain Monetti McAdam, head of the TINGEWICK[9] Mission, who was sick with malaria in a nearby village, having been forced to flee from his station by the movement of German tanks. He had sent an advance party to set up a new headquarters in a safer area, but was too sick to accompany them and decided to wait in the village of Prianza until he was well enough to travel which, thanks to the intervention of good medical care, he eventually was.[ix]

Arriving back at a 0400 from the Triklinos drop, the crew debriefed and grabbed some sleep before an evening take-off and a return to Greece with another agent, destined for the LAPWORTH Mission of Captain Wickstead in Pieria. When they arrived over the Katafygion dropping ground, there were no signal fires and they circled overhead for twenty minutes with all eyes straining to see the signals. Suddenly there they were – three fires in a line – followed five minutes later by one large red fire and a correct answer to the letter of the day. The drop was on and, after a dummy run, Tom came round again, lowered the flaps and slowed the aircraft to a shuddering 110 mph. The despatcher shouted 'Go' as the green light came on and the agent jumped out. Once on the ground, he flashed an

---

[9] British Mission operating with partisans in Agrinion area of Greece

agreed signal back to the crew to say that he was safe and they proceeded to drop the supplies in three further runs. The crew usually gave personnel the option of jumping first before the supplies, or going last on the final run, but the most important thing was to put them down in the right place. A crew member later commented: "You made damn sure you put them down in the right place or they might be a bit niggled when they got back". No pilot wanted to make life any more hazardous for these plucky men, who sat on the floor of the aircraft and on the signal to 'Go', shuffled sideways, swung their legs over the open hatch and dropped out into the black night. With the eight-hour mission safely accomplished, the crew returned to base, with the much-anticipated Squadron concert to look forward to that evening. After catching up on some sleep they headed for the specially-built stage at the fort, carrying their own petrol tins for seats and, as the parachute curtains opened, the footlights (a few borrowed light bulbs) shone on a hugely successful production, earning the organiser, Flying Officer Guest, a rousing cheer of appreciation from the troops.

A couple of days later a detachment of five crews – Fairweather, Harding, Storey, Dunphy and Fortune – accompanied Wing Commander Blackburn to Grottalgie in south-east Italy in an effort to deliver personnel and supplies to Tito's partisans in Yugoslavia's northerly dropping grounds. The reduced flying distance would mean less fuel and greater loads, but the downside was that Grottalgie was not set up for operating heavy bombers at night and basic amenities such as fuel, spares and lighting were not in place. This was no problem for the wing commander, whose organising ability and charismatic personality had the base operational within a week, though not without the occasional incident, of the 'Boy's Own' adventure kind. On one particular night, Tom had turned on to the airstrip and was about to take off when the electric runway lights all went out. They sat transfixed as German planes came in and bombed the airfield and the next thing they heard was a loud banging on the door of the aircraft and the wing commander's voice bellowing: "Get this bloody thing up in the air". Flight engineer Charlie Keen climbed out and lined them up with a couple of torches and off they went – "Everyone got up that night despite the bomb craters!"[x] The men thought very highly of the wing commander, who had far exceeded the number of operations required of an officer in his position and he led by example, insisting on being the first in the air every night, which meant catching up on his admin work into the early hours of the morning. It was said to be personal – James Blackburn's parents had been caught in Shanghai when the Japanese attacked and his commitment and sense of duty were extraordinary – he was an inspiration to the crews in his Squadron.

It was on the night of the 26th November 1943, whilst flying from the Grottaglie air base, that my father's Halifax lost a crew member – Peter Crosland. Comrades were lost on a regular basis, but the loss of Peter was different – he was one of them. They had taken off that night for a supply drop to Slovenia, where Major William Jones, head of the HUNDON Mission[10] Station, had sent an urgent request for twenty tons of explosives for his partisans, who were keen to destroy sections of the railway line between Ljubliana and Zagreb. Bad weather had prevented the supply drop two nights earlier and this was a second attempt for Halifax JN888 from the Grottaglie airstrip. On arriving at the Oklinak drop zone, Tom asked Walter Davis to break radio watch and help the despatcher to prepare the internal load and open the aperture doors ready for the drop. Bomb aimer Peter Crosland was feeling unwell, but as the aircraft circled, he remained in position, prone on his stomach, looking down in case the target appeared. They circled for more than an hour, the aperture

---

[10] HUNDON, later FLOTSAM, British Mission attached to Tito's Partisans in Slovenia

open in readiness for the drop, and then Crosland, twenty-years-of-age, requested permission to use the Elsan. "Not until we are clear of the target area," said Tom. Two minutes later Peter said: "I'll have to go!" at which point he was granted permission and made his way through the aircraft to the rudimentary chemical toilet at the back. Meanwhile Tom, having circled for an hour and forty minutes with no sign of fires, decided to abandon the drop and Walter was ordered back to his radio position to listen for broadcasts from other aircraft. Rear gunner, Jim Hughes requested permission to leave his turret and assist the despatcher and this was granted. Walter made his way back through the aircraft and, as he paused by the heater to warm up, he saw Peter help the despatcher to move the packages forward of the aperture. As he turned away, he caught a blurred movement out of the corner of his eye that made him look back.[xi] "Where's Peter?" he called out. In the cockpit, Tom, and Engineer Charlie Keen, had felt a sudden change of pressure in the aircraft and knew straight away that something, or someone, had gone out of the plane. A search of the aircraft was carried out but there was no trace of Peter, who had fallen out of the hatch wearing his life vest and parachute harness, but not the pack. The crew desperately checked the parachute packs, unable to believe what had happened, but all seven were accounted for and their worst fears were confirmed. Peter had hurtled out into the night from 1500 feet with no hope of survival.

His body lay where it fell, on a mountainside in the District of Cabar, on the Slovenia-Croatia border, for more than three years before it was finally found by a forest worker who removed his identity tags and buried him respectfully on the hillside. After the war, one of the RAF's MRES[11] searcher parties, operating in that area of Yugoslavia, was approached

---

[11] Missing Research and Enquiry Service (formed to investigate cases of missing airmen).

by the forester who had found the remains. He had kept the articles that identified the body and came running up to them saying: "I knew that one day the English would come back". He proudly handed over the tags and Peter's body was re-interred in the Belgrade War Cemetery.[xii] The Government of the time felt that our fallen should not be left in isolated cemeteries, but should rest in special War cemeteries, carefully chosen for their natural beauty and peace.[xiii] On that dark night in November, the crew only knew that he was gone and returned to base with their full load and heavy hearts – the entry in that night's log book DNCO (did not complete operation). Back in the billet, Peter's bed, with his gramophone and two records neatly stacked alongside, was empty. Empty beds the morning after operations could mean that a crew had ditched but were safe somewhere, or had run out of fuel and landed away from base, but in the case of Peter Crosland, aged 20, they knew he would not be back. He had fallen to his death on a filthy November night on to a cold mountain side. One of his two gramophone records was the song 'Goodbye' from the operetta The White Horse Inn,[12] and the crew had always laughed and sung along with the line: 'Where the desert sand is handy, we'll all be full of grit and you won't see our heels for the dust'. But now the song echoed with the hollow sound of loss:

'My heart is broken but what care I
Such pride inside me has woken
I'll try my best not to cry by and by
When the final farewells must be spoken'

The crew were devastated, but grateful that Squadron etiquette demanded that such incidents were not discussed with other crews, which eased their grief. The despatcher was affected

---

[12] Operetta The White Horse Inn, words and music by Ralph Benatzky and Robert Stolz

particularly badly and was looked after by Tom throughout the remainder of their first tour of duty. He then declined an immediate second tour with the other members of the crew. Walter Davis commented that it was later forbidden to volunteer for an immediate second tour as crews were becoming mentally disturbed by further duties.[xiv] A couple of nights after the tragedy, the crew were back in the skies for an attempt to drop five personnel to the SWIFTER Mission[13] in southern Albania, and although signal fires were seen at the drop zone, they were not in the pattern as briefed to the pilot before take-off, and with no reply seen to the flashed letter of the day, Tom decided that it was not safe to drop the personnel, and flew on to their secondary target of Koritsa to drop leaflets, after which they returned to the primary target. Eight fires were now lit, but still not in the shape of a cross, as briefed. They were sufficiently confident to drop the supplies as the topography matched the pinpoint, but the agents were returned to base.[xv] It was hazardous enough being dropped into a remote mountain region at night, but to drop without correct signals being received was too risky, as the fires were sometimes discovered and lit by the Germans in order to lure the aircraft in. Only the exchange of correct signals was acceptable for dropping personnel. Except that, on this occasion, the well-intentioned decision to return them to Tocra led indirectly to their deaths. Forty-eight hours later five personnel climbed into a Halifax of 624 Squadron, piloted by Flight Sergeant Dennis Howlett, and headed back to the SWIFTER Mission in Albania. Nothing more was heard of the aircraft, until the news began to trickle in that it had crashed in flames in Greece, killing all seven crew and the five agents.

These were active months for the infiltration of agents into the Balkans, many of whom were recruited from the armed

---

[13] British Mission working with established partisan bases in the mountains west of Korca in Albania

services, the 'old-boy network' or were nationals of the countries into which they were dropped. Once recruited, some of them underwent training in sabotage and survival in the incongruous setting of an English country house, followed by paramilitary training in the wild, empty spaces of Scotland, and finally parachute training. This was essential because they would be dropped into their assigned country under cover of darkness and usually at a remote and inaccessible location. A few went in 'blind' and would need to be completely self-sufficient and familiar with the terrain to get by, but the majority were dropped to a 'reception' group waiting on the ground. A handshake and a pat on the back must have been reassuring after jumping from an aircraft at night. Some didn't survive the descent and others disappeared altogether and were never heard of again. It was a dangerous business and these were not tough SAS types, but, for the most part, regular soldiers, patriots and idealists who had volunteered or were recruited for their specialist expertise, language skills or knowledge of the country involved. The task for personnel, once infiltrated, was to liaise with the most effective resistance groups and provide them with money, radios, leaders and weaponry. There was usually also a political dimension, unique to each country, which made their task very difficult. The British Cabinet were keen to ensure that Greece, whose King was in London, remained within the British sphere of influence after the war, and this was tricky for the agents in the field since only a minority in Greece wanted the King back at all and the groups most effectively fighting the enemy were republican or communist. Yugoslavia's King Peter was also in exile in London, and initially British missions were sent to support both Tito's communist and Mikhailovic's nationalist resistance fighters in that country. As 1943 drew to a close and with Churchill's direct emissary to Tito, Fitzroy Maclean, sending back positive reports of partisan effectiveness, it was decided that Tito would henceforth be the sole recipient of aid, and all further supplies were withdrawn from Mikhailovic, who, at best displayed a reluctance to attack German forces because of the inevitable reprisals on the community, and at worst was suspected of collaborating with the Germans.[14]

> "I can assure the House that every effort in our power will be made to aid and sustain Marshal Tito and his gallant band. The Marshal sent me a message during my illness, and I have since been in constant and agreeable correspondence with him. We intend to back him with all the strength we can draw, having regard to our other main obligations."(Churchill) [xvi]

At the end of November 1943, their first month of special-duty operations, the Storey crew had undertaken twelve sorties, of which five had been fully successful on primary targets. Weather conditions and lack of signals accounted for the failures, though leaflets were successfully dropped on most secondary targets, which didn't require the accuracy of a supply or agent drop. It was often the missions that were not completed (DNCO) that proved the most testing because they often involved circling over a target at low altitude for a long time before deciding to abort. The weather conditions in Europe during that winter of 1943/44 were terrible, and this put enormous strain on the young crews and also their aircraft. Three crew members in these early flights, Walter Davis, Charlie Keen and Jim Hughes had met at 10 Operational Training Unit in Abingdon, where, early in training, they were given the opportunity to 'crew up'. This was a fairly informal process during which they chose who to fly with and Walter remembered how he met Tom Storey and came to join the crew: "A very tall sergeant approached me to ask if I would be his wireless operator and could I pick out a good navigator.

---

[14] Allegations made against Mikhailovic were disputed by a number of Mission officers attached to him and the withdrawal of support to him and subsequent abandonment remains controversial.

I said I knew just the man."[xvii] Charlie Keen recalled many years later that, having agreed to join the crew as flight engineer, they went off to the cinema. When they came out of the show, Tom took hold of Charlie's arm and said: "I can't see a thing in the dark!" Charlie was taken aback, thinking – "What kind of mistake have I made here? I've crewed up with a pilot who has no night vision." But then Tom laughed and he realised it was a joke. In fact Charlie always maintained that Tom's landings were better at night than during the day, and since he flew forty-two operations with him, he was well qualified to judge! Team spirit was everything and the ex-policeman, the sheet-metal worker, the office clerk and the shop assistant not only flew together, but spent their off-duty hours together as well, forming a solid team. Now, at the end of November 1943, a month in which the men of 148 Squadron had given hope and practical support to resistance fighters throughout the Balkans, they began to make plans for the festive season. A committee, led by the ever resourceful Flying Officer Guest, was formed to make arrangements for the Christmas celebrations. They might be a long way from home, but a spirited approach to this traditional family time boosted morale.

Also at the end of November, Churchill, Stalin and Roosevelt were meeting secretly at the Soviet Embassy in Teheran, with Stalin in a strong negotiating position after Russia's crushing defeat of the German army at Stalingrad, and continued advance, which had created a significant turning point in the war. The leaders agreed to give Tito stronger allied support in Yugoslavia, and Stalin managed to extract tacit permission to manipulate Poland's border with Russia after the war and install puppet governments in other Baltic states, sealing the fate of Poland, Czechoslovakia and Romania for the next 50 years.

Chapter 2

CHRISTMAS AT TOCRA

High priority for the Squadron in early December was operation AUTONOMOUS – the infiltration of agents Alfred de Chastelain and Ivor Porter into Romania. Their mission, a political one, was to link up with opposition leader Iuliu Maniu and convince him of the need to accept an unconditional surrender to the Russians. An attempt had been made to get just de Chastelain in during the moonless part of the night of the 22nd November, using three aircraft, one carrying de Chastelain, and two simulating a mine-laying operation in the Danube to divert attention.[i] The attempt failed because of a thick cloud layer that obscured the drop zone, and whereas the two diversionary Halifaxes jettisoned their bombs over the sea and returned safely to base, the aircraft carrying de Chastelain became iced up on the return leg, ran out of fuel and crash-landed in the sea. Ivor Porter had been awake all night waiting for news of the mission and was feeling reasonably hopeful because of the favourable weather reports, but when the aircraft didn't return his optimism turned to anxiety. The next day news began to dribble in that de Chastelain and the crew had parachuted to safety but the aircraft was lost.[1]

---

[1] Ivor Porter, in his book 'Autonomous' says that the aircraft carrying de Chastelain in November was a Liberator, but the Squadron Records state that it was a Halifax, piloted by F/Lt Brotherton-Ratcliffe.

The Storey crew took part in the next attempt to get the AUTONOMOUS agents in, on the night of the 4/5th December, and this time five Halifax aircraft were involved, with Warrant Officer Cyril Fortune, described in the Squadron Operations Record Book as "Second to none on the Squadron for piloting and daring-do", carrying both de Chastelain and Ivor Porter. Three of the diversionary aircraft were to drop delayed-action bombs into the Danube, which would create a big splash and go off after a few hours, giving the illusion of prematurely-exploding mines. The Storey crew's role in the deception, as the fourth diversionary aircraft, was to drop leaflets over Sofia and Plovdiv in Bulgaria and cause as much mayhem as possible, to make it look as though they were diverting attention from the mine-laying and thus keeping everyone's attention off the personnel drop. As they circled over Sofia, wireless operator Walter Davis turned his 'identification friend or foe' (IFF) signal on and off to interfere with enemy radar and, with searchlights scanning the sky, they gave a conspicuous enough display to give the impression that they were deliberately diverting attention from something else! All was going to plan, but when Fortune's aircraft arrived at the target with de Chastelain and Porter, despite perfect visibility, there were no reception signals and the operation had to be abandoned again. Three of the aircraft had already completed their diversionary work so the fourth aircraft, which had been the last to take off, jettisoned her bombs over the sea on receipt of the prearranged 'abandon' signal, and they all headed back to base. Ivor Porter was bitterly disappointed at the failure of the plan, especially as they had been able to pick out lights in the windows of the houses on the ground, and yet they had received no signals:

> "This crew had put in many operational flying hours; the pilot was a quiet, impressive character in whom we had complete confidence; the weather had been better that one would expect for the time of year. A chance like this was unlikely to occur again."[ii]

On the return leg, all five aircraft were diverted to Benina because of strong crosswinds at Tocra, and Ivor Porter grumbled about having to spend the night in the plane: "Cold, hungry and angry". Agents must have had nerves of steel to endure these long flights with all the fear and anticipation involved only to have to return to base and go through it all again.

And they did go through it all again on the 21st December; Porter, de Chastelain and Romanian sabotage expert, Silviu Metianu. An experienced crew was assembled in a Liberator, piloted by Brotherton-Ratcliffe, and the three personnel were successfully dropped into southern Romania, just north of the Danube. They landed in a thick mist and had difficulty finding each other, but this was just the start of their troubles. They had come down fifteen kilometers from their intended target and couldn't find the car and driver that should have been waiting for them, so they hid overnight and walked to a nearby village the next morning to get some help. The villagers didn't help them – in fact they turned them over to the gendarmes, claiming a reward in the process, and the three men were taken into custody where they remained for the next nine months. They were eventually freed in August 1944 when King Michael, twenty-two years of age, carried out a remarkable act of political courage in deposing fascist dictator Antonescu, dismissing his government and finally putting Romania on the side of the Allies for the rest of the war.[iii]

Ivor Porter, in his memoirs written after the war, expressed irritation at the RAF's failed drops and navigational errors, which is probably natural for someone involved in such dangerous work. He said of the first attempt to get de Chastelain in: "The Liberator had stooged too long over the target looking for signals, their radio had broken down; they had mis-navigated over Albania, run short of fuel and had all baled out off the Italian coast."[iv] The aircraft was in fact a Halifax, and Brotherton-Ratcliffe was one of the most experienced and respected pilots in the Squadron. His version of events was that, on the return trip, the plane had become iced up – so much so that the noise of cracking ice was heard throughout the aircraft – and his instruments had flicked on and off, with the airspeed indicator sporadically reading zero. The flight engineer reported that they had used 300 gallons of fuel in 50 minutes, which was 75% more than normal, and he summed it all up on the official RAF 441A Form with remarkable understatement: "Operation not successful. Ran out of petrol over Italy after attempting to land in unsuitable conditions – crew baled out – aircraft lost."[v]

Weather conditions had once again led to a failed operation and contributed to the loss of an aircraft. It was, above all else, the biggest factor in failure rates during the winter months because, even if the aircraft reached the drop zone, the crew needed to see the ground and that meant coming down low to try and get beneath the clouds or, if amidst mountains, circling at a safe height in the hope of a window opening up. The Squadron would shortly bring into service the Rebecca/Eureka system of air-to-ground radar that improved the efficiency of drops, but for the moment they relied on eyesight. When it came to dropping personnel, even greater care was taken, and in the case of the AUTONOMOUS drop, additional precautions were taken to avoid drawing attention to the lead aircraft. The pilot was instructed to close and open the throttles of all four engines in order to give the reception committee an aural recognition signal. This was to be repeated several times and it was stressed to the crew that no visual signal must be given from the aircraft. They had nothing but respect for the personnel they carried and did their best to drop them at the optimum height and in the right place – "They were great blokes – they said nothing from the time we took off till they went out of the hole. They just got themselves ready and went – marvellous lads."[vi]

By December the Greek civil war was at its height and, although an immediate ban on the supply of arms to either side had initially been imposed, this was later lifted in respect of General Napoleon Zervas, leader of the republican EDES guerrilla movement who had proved loyal to the British and was seen as the non-aggressor, having been attacked first by ELAS.[2] Wing Commander Blackburn and Tom Storey delivered supplies for Zervas, at his Kalentzi headquarters, on the night of the 3rd December, and in spite of a confusion of dummy and true fires at the drop zone, both aircraft dropped their loads within ten minutes of each other in eight runs. Part of the understanding with the British was that Zervas should not use weaponry supplied to him by air to advance his cause in the civil war, but for the Allied officers attached to opposing ELAS guerrillas, this policy caused ill feeling and put them in a difficult and dangerous position.[vii] It was frustrating for Allied officers that while the Germans were burning villages throughout Greece, the partisan groups were keener to fight each other than the enemy. The partisans knew that it was only a matter of time before the Germans departed and, for them, the primary goal was to establish a position of superiority for when that time came. One man who worked hard on peace negotiations between the guerrilla factions was US Major Gerald Wines, who was dropped to the Allied Military Mission in Viniani by the Storey crew on the night of the 7th December. 'Jerry' Wines, veteran of World War I, became head of the American component of the Allied Military Mission, earning widespread respect for the solidarity he helped to foster between the British and Americans in Greece.[viii] It was he and Christopher Woodhouse who eventually persuaded the parties in the Civil War to sign a peace treaty and agree to assist with operation NOAH'S ARK, subsequently delayed, which was the sabotage and harrying of retreating Germans.[ix] The other members

---

[2] Greek People's Liberation Army.

of the OSS team dropped by Tom Storey that December night were Lieutenant Kermit Anderson, Lieutenant Robert Moyers, Lieutenant Nicholas Tryforos and Sergeant Spiros Kaleyias, whose various activities included sabotage, the building of airstrips, distribution of humanitarian aid to the Greek people and the thousands of Italian soldiers stranded in the mountains following the armistice, and, in the case of Robert Moyers, medical care. As a trained dentist and vet Robert Moyers became somewhat of a hero to the Greek people as he amputated limbs and performed lifesaving surgery, but as a dentist, his skills were apparently not in great demand.[x]

A high proportion of flights during December were to Albania, following the appointment of Brigadier Edmund 'Trotsky' Davies as head of the Allied Mission there. He had been dropped in by the Forester crew in October and the enlarged Mission required stores and personnel. Winter conditions meant that the timing couldn't have been worse for the supply effort required and, to add to the miserable conditions on the ground, a German drive had already caused staff at two Mission stations to flee. By mid-December Brigadier Davies and his SPILLWAY Mission were on the run themselves in bitter-cold conditions of driving rain and snow. Night after night they waited for promised supplies that didn't arrive, and the growing sense of abandonment led to understandable ill-feeling:

> "Had an explanation followed we would have understood, but space on the air was considered too precious for explanations. We always felt that it was not appreciated at our base how much work and preparation went into a reception and how much disappointment was felt when no plane arrived. At base they felt that we did not appreciate engine failures, bad weather and changes in policy of allotting aircraft."[xi]

The Storey and Ellison crews had managed to deliver rations, clothing, stores and explosives to the more southerly Mission[3] of Major Bill Tilman in November, but the next three drops attempted by the Storey crew failed because of either incorrect signals or engine trouble. Bill Tilman had been in Albania for four months, having arrived just before the Italian surrender, and he didn't think there would be much to do except perhaps help with the repatriation of Italian prisoners and try to stop the Albanians from massacring them. However, the swift movement of German troops into Albania made for a much tougher assignment, and although Tilman and his partisans did their best to slow the enemy's progress by burning bridges and attacking garrisons, they were powerless to prevent the large-scale burning of villages that accompanied the German progress. With the onset of winter and lack of supplies, conditions became very bleak. Relief came when the Brotherton-Ratcliffe crew managed to get one supply load to them in mid-December and another at the end of the month. Bill Tilman described in his memoir what it was like being on the receiving end of a supply drop:

> "It was a heartening sight to see a big four-engine Halifax roar down the valley five- or six-hundred feet over the signal fires, drop its load, do a tight turn without troubling to gain height, and come back for its second run. As the plane turned, the navigation lights on the wings seemed almost to brush the hillside."[xii]

There were too many times though when the supply drop failed and the frustration and disappointment of the reception group was also felt by the crews, who had flown for hours, only to arrive at the drop zone and find no visibility, no signal fires, or the wrong letter of the day flashed to them from the

---

[3] SCULPTOR.

ground. Sometimes the reception group lit dummy fires to divert enemy attention from the actual drop zone and the crew would need to be briefed not only on the correct signals, but also the dummies, which they would need to identify while controlling a low-level approach amidst shrouded mountain peaks. One of the most common medical problems suffered by pilots was visual fatigue, which is not surprising considering the level of concentration demanded of them, almost always in poor light.[xiii] The reception groups themselves were not always well organized as they waited furtively on the ground, exposing themselves to danger by lighting fires, only to then hear the heavy drone of the aircraft circling above a dense cloud bank. Sometimes the aircraft would fly on to a secondary target and then return to the original one for another try, only to find that the fires had burned out and the partisans had given up, thinking the aircraft had gone. Enemy spotter planes were always on the lookout for the scorched earth of burned-out signal fires, which added to the danger for the reception group and encouraged the location of dropping grounds to be as remote and inaccessible as possible. A DNCO[4] in the logbook meant a failed operation, but that belied the effort and skill that a crew had put into the sortie, and, as they debriefed and headed for bed, the ground crew would get busy unloading the containers and bundles to prepare another aircraft for the next attempt. Each month a 'league table' would highlight success- or failure-rates for each crew, along with tables of tonnage dropped to each area and a breakdown of the reasons for failure – weather, mechanical, lack of signals, etc., all of which increased the pressure on the exhausted crews – nobody wanted to fail. These are fairly typical signals from the field:

"GUNLESS GASLESS FOODLESS WHY THIS DELAY – STOP – HURRY"[xiv]

---

[4] Did not complete operation.

"THIS IS TERRIBLE – STOP – ONE THOUSAND MEN WITHOUT AMMO HAVE WAITED THREE WEEKS FOR A DROP"[xv]

And the tetchy messages that went back displayed little sympathy:

"APPARENTLY YOU HAVE NO IDEA OF SORTIE POSITION. YOU ARE ONE OF MANY MISSIONS ON IMPORTANT TARGETS AND WEATHER BETWEEN AERODROME AND YOU IS BAD. PROPORTION SORTIES YOU VERY HIGH. UP TO YOU MAKE 'TEMPO' UNDERSTAND THIS.[xvi]

Supply drops were a lifeline for Mission personnel, not only bringing arms, food and clothing, but letters from home and news of the outside world. The SPILLWAY Mission in Albania, waiting at a cold drop zone with their restive pack mules, desperately needed food, winter clothes and ammunition, but most of all they wanted the letters, newspapers and books from home that they knew would be in No.1 container. Brigadier Davies later recalled that the priority following a drop was to retrieve the precious No.1 container, drag it over to a mule, load it and take it straight to the mess hut before it could be mislaid or stolen. Invariably the catches and hinges would have been damaged during the drop and so someone in the mess hut would hack at it with hammer and chisel to get at the longed-for letters from home.[xvii]

Theft from the containers and bundles was a very real problem because villagers in the vicinity of a drop zone soon learned to spot the signs of preparation for aircraft reception and made their way to the area in the dark, helping themselves to the contents of stray containers, which could be scattered over a wide area. The most highly prized was the bullion container, which the resourceful local folk soon learned to identify, leading Mission staff in Greece to start taking bright Aldis lamps to the reception area, switching them on after a drop to deter pilferers. A typical load for a Halifax on a supply run would be fifteen pre-packed containers for arms, ammunition and explosives, nine of which were stored in the fuselage bomb bay and three beneath each wing. These were released by the bomb-aimer to descend on parachutes, plus in the aircraft fuselage were an additional twenty to thirty packages and bundles given free drop, and around 230lbs of leaflets. These would be stacked to a considerable height in the fuselage and moved to either side of the dropping hatch by the despatcher during the flight. The despatcher, assisted by the wireless operator, worked in complete darkness to ensure that no light escaped through the bomb bay, and he would watch for a green light on his display board. This was the signal to push out the packages as fast as possible. A red light on his board would tell him to stop and, if any packages were left, the aircraft would do further runs until all the supplies had been dropped.

The rear gunner, in his cramped turret at the back of the aircraft would watch the packages as they left the aircraft to make sure they were dropping on the target. The strenuous nature of moving the large weight of stores, coupled with a lack of oxygen if the aircraft was flying above 10,000ft to avoid bad weather, imposed quite a strain on the despatchers' lungs, and the Squadron's medical officer was sufficiently concerned about the conditions that he flew on a sortie as second despatcher to see for himself what it entailed. He found the work exhausting and went on to recommend that despatchers should be rested whenever possible and spare aircrew brought in to relieve them.[xviii] In the early days, the crew had no idea what was in the containers and packages, but later they were alerted to very dangerous or valuable items, which could then be packed in such a way that they could be isolated if it became necessary to jettison the load. Bomb aimer, Eddie Elkington-Smith remembered bullion containers always going on number three bomb bay, and he could then be sure to keep that one with the aircraft, though Walter remembered an occasion when they jettisoned their entire load in the Adriatic, unaware of the contents. On returning to base they were told that they had jettisoned a container of bullion. The general rule for aircraft in trouble was not to jettison the load if they had been airborne for more than three hours, but anything less than that was at the pilot's discretion.

For the returning aircrews, there was little in the way of comfort at the Tocra base with persistent winter rain turning the camp into a sea of mud. The trench Tom and his crew had dug around their tent proved inadequate and the first real downpour washed their belongings out into the mud. Walter Davis described their next trench as resembling a "fenland dyke." It kept the rain out of the tent but also caught the occasional airman weaving his way back from the nearby Sergeants' mess to his own tent.[xix] One or two resourceful airmen had replaced their sand floors with concrete to try and make life tolerable but it wasn't long before the commanding officer, who attributed the scrounging of building materials to: "bad habits picked up in the desert", put up stern notices forbidding it. The airmen continued to occupy the tents, but the mess was now a permanent building and Nissen huts were erected for operational use, with officers moved to an empty fort nearby. The poor sanitary conditions were slowly being improved, thanks to an NCO sanitation squad, and a fumigator was made available in the sick quarters so that airmen could: "have their blankets fumigated, on request, daily after 1400 hrs".[5] Desert sores, skin infections stomach upsets and visual fatigue were the commonest medical conditions during this last quarter of 1943, but morale was surprisingly good considering the number of casualties and

---

[5] 148 Squadron ORB Summary 17th December 1943

the number of aircraft written off.[xx] Tom and his crew had a narrow escape on the night of the 15th December during a leaflet drop for the Political Warfare Executive, when a burst of flak came up through the clouds from the north-west end of Crete and made six or seven holes in the aircraft. The crew found it somewhat galling to come under fire from the ground for the sake of leaflets, but propaganda was part of the war effort and it was the despatcher's job to make sure that the correct language batch went out at each location.

Some credit for the morale of the Squadron must go to the social committee, led by Flying Officer Guest, who worked hard to organize concerts, whist drives, films and seasonal events. Christmas plans were certainly gathering pace and, at a meeting in the airmen's mess, it was agreed that lunch would take place in the central hall followed by buffet dinners at every section's canteen. Meanwhile, the mobile cinema was proving so popular that there were now two showings a day and, even then, demand could not always be met. For crews grounded by the weather there were long hours to kill, and during December a number of football matches took place, cooks versus electricians, or squadron versus maintenance crews. The airmen were just one part of the team of men working at the base. Meals had to be prepared, containers and bundles packed, aircraft maintained, supplies brought in, intelligence gathered and communications maintained. Flight crews, however, were on the front line, and when an aircraft failed to return, everybody felt it.

The Storey crew had not been flying on the night of 10th December, but were woken up by the sound of exploding ammunition from Halifax BB344 ('Fortune's Coleen'), which was engulfed in flames on the runway. The catalogue of disasters for Cyril Fortune and his crew that night began during the flight when, midway between changing places with the second pilot, violent turbulence flipped the aircraft upside down and dropped it 5,000ft before Fortune was able to regain control. Then, as they came in to land, the aircraft swung and ploughed into a parked spitfire, bursting into flames. Patrick Stradling, a member of Fortune's crew, was instrumental in saving their lives that night and, a few months later, when Stradling was missing and his fate unknown, Cyril Fortune wrote a wonderfully heartening letter to his parents to say that there was a very good chance he was safe and adding: "He was always a member of my crew and on one occasion he helped, with two others, to save us all from a very nasty situation, and for that I always felt proud and grateful".[xxi]

Poor weather conditions kept all Squadron aircraft grounded in the days leading up to Christmas and this gave the crews a well-earned break from flying. One of the Storey crew took a photograph of Halifax JN888, in which Tom and the crew had completed twenty-four sorties. Tom, with his floppy, curly hair looks out of the open window above a beautifully painted unicorn on the fuselage and the name 'RITA' on the nose, along with a star for every sortie flown. It was Walter, the

Halifax JN888 (Rita) taken at Tocra, December 1943

crew's wireless operator, who had created this masterpiece, making his own stencil so that he could add a star for every operation, and although personalization of aircraft was discouraged, it was often overlooked in the interests of crew morale. Before flying out to Libya Tom had been living with his new wife, Rita, at the family run Unicorn Hotel in Ludlow, and the bold artwork must have given him heart on the long walk out to his aircraft, before climbing into the cockpit to begin his pre-flight checks.

Halifax JN888, 'Rita', with her prancing unicorn artwork, only had seven months of flying left. She crashed in the Pyrenees on the 13th July, 1944 while supplying French Resistance fighters, and was just four miles from the drop zone; her crew having flown her over 600 miles by dead reckoning. Pilot Officer Leslie Peers of the Royal Canadian Air Force and his crew died at the scene. The Mayor of the nearby village of Nistos wrote in 1945:

> "The seven occupants of the plane were killed instantly. A shepherd found them on the 15th July. At once a large group of inhabitants of Nistos went to the scene and there buried the seven heroes. They dug seven graves side-by-side and buried the heroes in beds of fern. It was impossible to take coffins there because the place was two-and-a-half hours walk away amongst precipitous mountains, and moreover this country was occupied by the enemy. We erected a wooden fence round their small cemetery and a cross, also of wood, bears the inscription: *To the memory of our heroic allies, who died for France. Their graves will not be left untended.*"[6]

In stark contrast to the story of this crash is the loss of Halifax HR674 on the night of 19/20 October 1943. SAPLING 7 was

---

[6] Their sacrifice is also commemorated on the Runnymede Memorial.

a personnel and supply drop to the Albanian Mission of Major Jerry Fields. Flight Lieutenant Forester knew the Albanian drop zones well and had, just a few days earlier, taken Brigadier 'Trotsky' Davies's SPILLWAY Mission into the Chermenika mountains, noting on his crew's map of the drop zone: 'Climb quickly, left-handed, or else'.[xxii] On that fateful night the reception party lit the signal fires only to hear the "scream of the engines"[7] as the Halifax came in low and crashed into the mountainside, killing all on board, including two men destined to join the Mission. The terrible phrase: "scream of the engines" describes all too graphically the desperate efforts of the pilot as he uses maximum thrust to try and prevent the inevitable. When Field went down to bury the dead, the Albanian partisans, for whom the supplies were intended, "proved more interested in looting and grumbling that their material was lost and would not help to dig the graves". Field was helped in this task by a group of Italian soldiers and two old men. He was very disillusioned at the waste of British life on behalf of the Albanians who did not appreciate the sacrifice, and he never got over it. In a report in 1943 he wrote: "Hate the country and hate the people. We will of course continue to do our best, but if there is any excuse for another type of work and evacuation from here, we should jump at it."[xxiii]

The crew of Halifax HR674 had been familiar with the Albanian drop zones and their loss, which has never been fully explained, illustrates the danger that all Special Duty pilots faced. The partisans chose remote areas as drop zones – small valleys enclosed by mountains and, in the darkness, what might appear to be a hole safe to use for descent, could well be a hilltop or protruding mountain peak. I remember Charlie Keen telling me that on some drops, particularly in

---

[7] Words of eyewitness Austin DeAth (from The Wildest Province, Roderick Bailey, Page 195)

Yugoslavia, the heavy aircraft, laden with supplies, would have to spiral down inside a bowl of mountains, do a low-level drop and then spiral out again. He recalled the steady voice of the navigator over the intercom as they came in for the final approach: "you can do it Tommy, you can get in there." Mechanical failure or a fire at this stage of a drop (which is what was suspected for the SAPLING crash) could only have one outcome.

At Tocra the general stand-down of operations and arrival of Christmas meant a rare opportunity for the crews to relax and enjoy three days of well-planned festivities, starting with much drinking in all section canteens, which had been specially decorated with Christmas trees and streamers, followed by midnight mass in the HQ Block. Christmas Day was a complete stand-down for everyone except the duty pilot, but even he was given three hours off to have his Christmas lunch of 'Crème a la Tomato, Roast Turkey and Xmas Pudding'.[8] Buffet dinners in the various sections that evening were visited by both the outgoing Wing Commander Blackburn, and the incoming Wing Commander Pitt, with much good cheer all round. Walter Davis, who was 'duty pilot' that day, remembered that the mess staff had been hosted by the officers during the course of the day, and were rather the worse-for-wear by the time it came to providing supper in the Sergeants' mess. He described the meal as "a rather poor effort!"[9] Nevertheless, a convivial atmosphere prevailed as they signed each other's menu cards with good humoured messages. Pat Stradling, who carried his signed menu card in his wallet long after the end of the war, got a note from Paddy Fortune: "Good luck to you and many thanks for help in a dangerous position". And from Jack Easter, wireless operator on the Fortune crew: "Your smiling mug on the other side

---

[8] Menu preserved by Patrick Stradling
[9] My Grandad's Story, a Memoir, Walter Davis and Sharon Spencer

of the hole is always a great help to me – good dropping". Tom Storey, whose crew he would join in a couple of months, wrote: "For pete's sake, don't forget to let go Paddy."[xxiv] The following day, as the weather stand-down continued, a Squadron Concert Party was held in the concert hall, and so ended Christmas 1943 at Tocra airbase. A crew change saw Canadian Oscar 'Hap' Congdon join the crew as navigator, replacing Flying Officer Nichol, and the crews of 148 Squadron prepared for a January move to Brindisi, on the south-east coast of Italy.

CHAPTER 3

148 SQUADRON MOVES TO BRINDISI

"There is not the slightest prospect of finding suitable weather for dropping on any of the available areas tonight," was the view of the Met Officer, Flight Lieutenant Rowles, as the New Year began, and it wasn't much better the following night, with operations limited to areas north of Latitude 43N. Consequently six aircraft were briefed for Serbia and took off at nightfall with supplies for MULLIGA-TAWNY, the Mostyn Davies Mission, which had been making its way to the Bulgarian border, dodging hostile German, Bulgar, and Albanian forces, and up against the most atrocious winter conditions. This doomed operation was being stoically endured on the ground by a handful of brave men who, on this cold January night, would wait in vain for their air-drop of supplies. All six aircraft failed, either because the cloud cover was too thick, the signals, when spotted, were incorrect, or in the case of Tom Storey's Halifax, because of mechanical trouble. "Altogether a very abortive night," was the summary in the ORB[1] for that night. Tom's aircraft had climbed continuously after take-off to try and get above the dense cloud layer, but icing at 14,000ft prevented them getting any higher and, as they began to descend, the elevator stick jammed forward and stayed jammed until they got down

---

[1] Operations Record Book. Every Squadron kept a record log and a summary log of operations

to 5000ft, when it finally released.[2] Engineer Charlie Keen then noticed that the oil-pressure had dropped and, suspecting that the excessive vibration from the jammed elevators had caused a leak, Tom decided to return to base, where this was confirmed by the ground crew.

The following day, as the crew caught up on some sleep in preparation for a 1730 take off to Albania, another drama was unfolding close to base. A Wellington of 38 Squadron had failed to return to its base near Benghazi, and a call came into 148 Squadron to see if it had landed at Tocra. It had not, but later in the day two Arabs arrived at the officers' mess bringing a message from one of the Wellington crew to say that they had crashed on an escarpment along the coast at Ptolomais, and urgently needed medical assistance. Flight Lieutenant Scott, the medical officer, raced off in his ambulance to the crash site to find one crew member dead and the others injured, the aircraft having apparently flown into a hillside in the dark. 38 Squadron was involved in reconnaissance and anti-submarine operations from their base at Berka, (Benghazi, Libya) and January was to be a bad month for them with the loss of two Wellington crews just a few days later.

JN888 was barely airborne for Albania that afternoon when a mechanical problem[3] forced Tom to abandon the flight for a second night running. For pilots, the decision of whether to plough on regardless with engine failure was one they were required to make on a regular basis. A Halifax could fly on three engines and so the decision would need to take a number of factors into consideration – height, weight of load, strength of headwinds, terrain at the drop zone, distance from base, and the likelihood of encountering night fighters, which would find

---

[2] Elevator flaps control the aircraft's orientation by changing the pitch of the aircraft, i.e. they make the aircraft nose-up or nose-down.
[3] Sheared reduction gear.

the slow-manoeuvring aircraft an easy target.[i] An inner-engine failure would make it difficult to hold course with the aircraft skidding through the air, losing performance and manoeuvrability. An outer-engine failure would increase these effects, so that the pilot would have to fly 'hands on' – something that required real physical effort. The exhausted pilot flying like this for many hours on the homeward flight would not then be at his best for a three-engine night landing. Tom was lucky on this occasion in that the engine failure occurred early in the flight, making the decision to turn back possible. Flight Lieutenant Brotherton-Ratcliffe and his crew were not quite so lucky when, a few nights later, they suffered double engine failure close to their dropping ground on the Greek-Albanian border. They lost the outer engine on the way to the drop but continued, only to lose the inner engine on the same side as they manoeuvred in mountainous terrain for their second drop. Flight Lieutenant Morris, the navigator, guided his skipper through the twists and turns of the valley but, trapped in between mountains, they were forced to turn to the dead-engine side, which increased the rate of descent and, with no hope of gaining height, the crew baled out, leaving Brotherton-Ratcliffe to crash-land the aircraft in a field. The crew destroyed the aircraft as instructed and were then whisked away to a hideout in the hills by Captain Ian Hamilton, an agent they had dropped on a previous operation.[ii] It was only a matter of weeks since this same crew had jumped to safety from their Halifax after the failed AUTONOMOUS drop with de Chastelain, and to hear that against all the odds the entire crew had survived another such incident must have given heart to their fellow crews at Brindisi. They spent ten weeks in Albania, eventually making it back to Brindisi in a motor torpedo boat, with the swashbuckling Brotherton-Ratcliffe sporting a huge ginger beard, and looking very much the guerrilla fighter he had become.

Activities back at base were now focused on the impending move to Italy and all leave was cancelled from the second week of January. The final operation from Tocra for the Storey crew was another attempt to drop supplies to Mostyn Davies and his MULLIGATAWNY Mission, which was now very close to the Bulgarian border, having walked through the mountains with their pack mules for eleven weeks, battered by wind, rain and snow and badly in need of supplies. The Chalk and Harding crews had been the last to get supplies to them on the 20th December, but the noise of the aircraft had caught the attention of the Bulgarians and the team on the ground were caught up in a skirmish, which forced them to bury most of their stores and move on[iii]. Now, on the 18th January, five aircraft were heading back to the desolate border region of Eastern Serbia to drop supplies and infiltrate a support Mission by the name of CLARIDGE, comprising Major Frank Thompson and Signalman Watts, who were to be dropped at the same Dobro Polje dropping ground. With Thompson and Watts on board the Fortune aircraft and the Storey, Edwards, Harding and Botham crews carrying supplies, they each arrived over the target to find thick cloud-cover, and none of them were able to spot signal fires. Tom descended to 7000ft in an attempt to get below the cloud, but decided to abort when he spotted a mountain peak penetrating the cloud layer. He would not have seen the fires anyway because they had not been lit, owing to a mix-up between Cairo and the Mission, and all five aircraft turned back and landed at Brindisi. JN888 was declared unserviceable after the sortie and the crew returned to base as passengers on the Edwards aircraft, leaving JN888 to be flown back to Tocra a couple of days later by Group Captain Rankin, officer commanding 334 Wing, who was busy making arrangements for the Squadron move to Brindisi. The ferrying of stores, equipment, and personnel now began in earnest, with the Halifax crews making a couple of trips each, and Flight Lieutenant Tupper in the Squadron's Liberator, making eighteen trips. Most of the personnel were transported this way, with the remainder going by sea. The upheaval meant that there was no operational flying at all between the 22nd and

31st January. So with 148 Squadron out of action, it was down to 624 Special Duty Squadron to drop the CLARIDGE Mission of Thompson and Watts, and this they did on the 25th January, with the aircraft of Pilot Officer Garnet carrying the personnel and two further aircraft carrying the supplies for MULLIGATAWNY[iv]. As these crews arrived back at their Brindisi base having successfully completed the operation, a new crew had just arrived from England – that of Flight Sergeant Edward Tennant, whose time with the Squadron was to be tragically short.

Further supplies for MULLIGATAWNY and CLARIDGE were flown in by the Storey, Fairweather, and Chalk crews when the Squadron resumed operations at the beginning of February, but this minor relief could not save MULLIGATAWNY and CLARIDGE from complete disaster. Apart from the impossible task of supplying these operations adequately over the winter months, the strength of partisan support had been misjudged, and they met with strong opposition, which they were unprepared for. They had been set an impossible task. Mostyn Davies was killed in a skirmish the following month and, although Frank Thompson narrowly escaped on that occasion, he was wounded and captured very soon after when he moved over the border into Bulgaria with his partisan group. He was later shot by firing squad, along with his partisan leaders and villagers who had helped them. The entire MULLIGATAWNY Mission, with their courageous leader Mostyn Davies, perished in Bulgaria, as did the young Frank Thompson of CLARIDGE Mission.

The Fairweather crew, who had brought relief to that embattled Mission, were themselves killed just five months later on a disastrous night when the Squadron lost four crews, including that of Squadron Leader Surray Bird. Tom Fairweather's Halifax JP292 was hit by a Dornier night fighter over Serbia, and one of the pilots flying that night, Jack Pogson, recalled seeing the flashes away in the distance as the Halifax (which he had flown with to the dispersal point) came under attack from German night fighters. "They were catching hell", said Jack, who had moved away from the formation and was heading for his target in Poland. Squadron Leader Bird, in Halifax JP286, had been carrying the four-man DEERHURST Mission, into Hungary, and had safely dropped the agents before being hit by a Messerschmitt night fighter on the homeward leg. The DEERHURST team were to link up with a resistance group north-west of Lake Balaton, and although they were dropped before the aircraft was hit, they landed alongside a Jewish Labour Camp and were rounded up by the guards, who subsequently handed them over to the Gestapo.[v] They managed to convince the Germans that they were paratroopers and, after interrogation, were sent to a POW camp for airmen, Stalag Luft VIII at Limburg. Two of the men were later killed in an Allied bombing raid on a rail yard whilst being transported by train.[vi] The bodies of the Fairweather crew, all less than twenty-five years of age, were recovered by German forces and eventually interred in the Belgrade War Cemetery.[vii] Squadron Leader Bird, aged twenty-four, and his crew are buried in the Budapest War Cemetery.[viii]

With the move to Brindisi complete, the most pressing problem for the airmen was overcrowding. The priority had been to get the runway serviceable, and the construction of wooden huts by the Italian labour-force was a long way behind schedule. The first arrivals were once again put up in tents and left to construct their own beds from a frame, some wire and mattress material.[ix] Wireless Technician Roger Alves took a photograph of the tented camp, with his Agfa Billy Zero camera, which captures better than any words the living conditions for airmen on arrival at Brindisi. In an attempt to maintain a basic level of hygiene, airmen were ordered to shake their blankets and put them out in the sun for at least two hours a day and each man was to take responsibility for

Tented Camp at Brindisi taken by Roger Alves
(Photo courtesy of Steve Alves)

the cleanliness of his bed space and take it in turns to clean the rest of the floor. The Medical Officer commented, in his Report for February 1944, that "Officers mostly have hired Italians to do the cleaning!"[4] The men were rationed to one bath a week and sanitary facilities were very basic, but they were now quite used to a level of discomfort and the temperate Italian climate combined with the proximity of Brindisi town and its ice-cream parlour were a definite improvement. Flying rations however were a sore point with the crew, and in February, the senior medical officer, having had frequent chats with aircrews on the subject, made an official report on the unsatisfactory situation:

"Considering the type of work and the long flying hours, rations are very unsatisfactory as regards quality and quantity. A small packet of biscuits, often stale, small slab of chocolate and a packet of chewing gum, in my opinion, do not constitute sufficient rations for a flight of anything up to eight hours."

---

[4] Medical Officer 148 Squadron, History of the War for February 1944 (AIR49/223)

Security was a further consideration as there were still a few unfriendly elements in Brindisi town, and pilfering from the airbase was a constant problem. The men were issued with revolvers for their personal safety and warned to be vigilant, but, despite the difficulties, morale was good. They were delighted to be out of the Libyan Desert, and looked forward to the challenge of new routes and destinations. The Air Ministry had recently ruled that the Squadron was to be known in future as 148 (Special Duties) Squadron, though under no circumstances were the men to mention this in any private correspondence.

When flying recommenced on the 1st February 1944, the Squadron came under 334 Wing, and a change of policy meant that Poland became the top priority, followed by the Italian partisans in northern Italy, and lastly the Balkans,[x] many of whose supply drops were now being undertaken by the American 62 Group and their shorter-range C47 transport aircraft. Operating from Brindisi would mean a much more efficient supply-run to the Balkans, reducing a seven-hour round trip to Albania to three hours, and extending the range of the Halifax further into the Italian Alps and to Poland. One of the early drawbacks proved to be the single runway, which was very susceptible to strong crosswinds, and a number of aircraft were damaged in the tricky conditions. Despite this, on the first night of operations from the new base, ten of the eleven serviceable aircraft set off for Balkan targets, and all but two were successful. The Storey crew destination that first night out of Brindisi was Croatia, and a supply-drop to the GEISHA Mission that was attached to Tito's partisans. Tito's presence loomed large during this period and, with Churchill's direct emissary Fitzroy Maclean attached to his Headquarters, supplies to partisans were given high priority. Tito himself, now Marshal of Yugoslavia, had been forced out of his Jajce Headquarters in January by a German drive and had set up a temporary camp in a the woods en route to Drvar, where he would establish a new base. Fitzroy Maclean, who had been visiting Cairo, returned to the Tito camp at this point, taking with him not only a personal letter from Churchill, but Churchill's son Randolph. Unable to land at their usual airstrip, which was in the hands of the Germans, they decided to parachute in to Bosanski Petrovac, in Bosnia, and for this purpose two experienced despatchers[5] were borrowed from 624 Squadron to help 'despatch' the party of seven. They flew in daylight, their Dakota escorted by twelve Thunderbolt fighter aircraft and accompanied by two Italian bombers carrying additional supplies.[xi] To parachute in during daylight hours and with such an escort was almost unprecedented and emphasised the priority given to the Maclean[6] Mission and the high regard in which Tito was held. Churchill delivered a speech the following month to the House of Commons, praising the partisan leader in glowing terms. It was therefore somewhat embarrassing that the BBC continued to call Tito 'General', when he had in fact been elevated to 'Marshal of Yugoslavia' by the communist-led resistance in November 1943. A signal from Maclean's Mission in late January 1944 read:

> "Why does BBC always call Tito General and not Marshal?"

Followed up three weeks later by:

> "Have still received no answer to question
> BBC still call Tito General
> Can you find whether acting on instructions from F/O
> [Foreign Office] and if so reason for these instructions."[xii]

Tito, in his woodland camp, was more concerned about practical matters – many of his men were marching through

---

[5] Flight Sergeant Roy Moller and Flight Sergeant Jim Rosebottom.
[6] MACMIS.

the winter snow with nothing but rags wrapped around their feet, and he was naturally preoccupied with the supply of boots so that his men could be mobilised and their hardship eased. A series of exchanges between Cairo and the GEISHA Mission in Croatia between 22nd and 30th January shows the priority given to Tito's request:

> 22nd: "Tito has ordered boots with overriding priority above other sorties..."

> 29th: "Explosives for you are high priority after immediate loads of boots. On specific instructions from Tito, boots RPT boots must be delivered before all else..."

> 30th "Fully appreciate lack sorties your area. Boots are only priority at moment on Tito's specific request. We are fixing explosive loads for you as soon as boots are exhausted..."

> 31st: "Tito's boot sorties almost cleared then explosives to you top priority..."

So it must have been some relief to the GEISHA Mission when, on the 1st February, the Storey, Fairweather, Edwards and Chalk crews arrived overhead at Zvecevo, near the Hungarian border, with their supplies and the long-awaited explosives. As for the boots, because of a shortage of Allied aircraft, some were dropped by an Italian Savoia-Marchetti bomber, which was in service as an Allied supply aircraft following the armistice. Fitzroy Maclean remembered one of these drops because, along with the boots, the aircraft delivered Andrew Maxwell of the Scots Guards, a personal friend of his, who apparently: "Dropped from a great height, followed by a free-drop of several hundred pairs of boots, which had passed him at high speed, missing him by inches".[xiii] Maxwell was lucky on that occasion, but a few months later a member of

Basil Davidson's SAVANNA[7] reception group was killed when a sack of boots, free-dropped from a Halifax, thudded down on to him as he waited by the fires.[xiv]

Balkan targets benefitted from the poor weather conditions during the first two weeks of February because, when sorties planned for the priority targets in northern Italy were cancelled by the Met Officer, all available aircraft were switched to Balkan operations, which was the case on the 10th February when the Storey crew were one of four given a SPINSTER[8] supply drop north of the Drin river. The crews were briefed on a primary and secondary target within the same area, the drops being for Wing Commander Tony Neel[9] in one valley and for Squadron Leader Arthur 'Andy' Hands in a neighbouring valley. Confusion at the reception end of the drop meant that when Neel's group heard aircraft overhead and raced to the top of the hill to dig their fires from under the snow and get them alight, they found that Hands already had his fires burning and was receiving all the supplies. Things were not much better for the aircraft overhead. The Dunphy crew, the first to arrive, reported being fired on from the ground during the drop and although the Storey and Aldred crews dropped without incident, Warrant Officer Pitt in Halifax JN956, who arrived later, also reported machine-gun fire aimed at his aircraft and abandoned the task. The last crew to take off for this area of Albania was that of Flight Sergeant McGugan, in Halifax JN959, and they did not return. Seven crew members, four of whom were Australian, died that night and are buried at the Belgrade War Cemetery. The only survivor was Sergeant Elkes, who was captured and became a prisoner

---

[7] Mission attached to Tito's partisans in the Vojvodina region of Yugoslavia (bordering Hungary)

[8] Albanian Mission headed by Squadron Leader Arthur 'Andy' Hands, based (in December 1943) in hills above the northern bank of the River Drin.

[9] Head of Albanian SLENDER Mission

of war. Unaware of the night's drama in the skies, Captain John Hibberdine, who, with Neel, had struggled to get the signal fires alight only to wait in vain for supplies, vented his frustration at the day's events in a diary entry: "We all left the dropping ground in a towering rage. To crown it all, the dog peed under Tony's bed and Otter (wireless op) was found amid a dismantled wireless set trying to persuade it to work."[xv] If they were feeling the strain of the situation it is not surprising; just days later, the Germans moved in and, with the local population turning against them, they were forced to gather what belongings they could and move west, spending the next two weeks on the run.

A crew change in February brought Eddie Elkington-Smith to the crew as bomb aimer and second pilot and, during his introduction to the crew, Tom's words went something like this: "My crew at the next table know this already, but you are new so let me say to you that, here on the ground I will be a great pal to you, but up there in the sky it is just discipline and discipline again. I will require it and I don't care what you think of me." Eddie, himself an old hand having completed twenty-six operations, was unimpressed with the 'new boy' lecture and tried to speak, but Tom came back: "Don't interrupt", and went on to introduce the crew one-by-one. A bit of playful banter then developed with Walter, the most religious of the group being described by Tom as the 'closest to God'. To which Walter muttered under his breath: "Well, God even likes policemen", referring to Tom's pre-war profession. "Yes, and look at me now", said Tom. "I used to be a policeman in the Midlands and here I am a volunteer in the service of His Majesty." Much laughter followed and, with the introductions made, Tom winked at the crew "Come on, let's get lucky. Time for a drink and I'm buying."[xvi]

Tom Storey was probably typical of many Royal Air Force Volunteer Reserve (RAFVR) pilots who found their way into the bomber squadrons, in that he was a young man who had done well at school and was at the start of his working life with all the optimism and idealism of youth. His dream, on leaving home, had been to make it as a professional footballer, but that didn't happen and instead, like his father before him, he did the sensible thing and joined the police force as a constable. A posting to Ludlow in Shropshire led him to a new life and to his wife to be, Rita. He played football for the town in his off-duty hours and grew to love his adopted home – a fondness that was reciprocated. He was unusually tall with wild curly hair, sometimes smoothed down with Brylcream, and kind blue eyes. A quietly spoken Cumbrian, he loved football, life, and most of all Rita. They had a song that they sang together. Tom would start and Rita would join in:

> "With someone like you, a
> pal so good and true,
> I'd like to leave it all behind
> and go and find
> Some place that's known to
> God alone,
> Just a spot to call our own."

Tom and Rita on their wedding day, July 1943

It was wartime and Ludlow was a town buzzing with the ebb and flow of military personnel stationed nearby. Tom went off to join the RAF in April 1941 and Rita joined the Women's Auxiliary Air Force as a wireless operator, proving herself particularly fast and accurate when it came to receiving Morse code messages. So, after initial training in Newcastle, she was posted to the wireless station at Chicksands Priory, where she spent long hours receiving messages to pass to the

Bletchley Park code-breaking team. They were both part of the war effort.

> "We'll find perfect peace, where joys never cease
> Out there beneath a kindly sky
> We'll build a sweet little nest, somewhere in the west
> And let the rest of the world go by"[10]

For Tom, the RAF gave him the opportunity to fly in every respect. He went to Canada to do his initial training and life became full of new and interesting experiences – he loved it, and felt a real sense of purpose. The invisible ceiling that tended to keep young men like him in trade and commercial jobs had been lifted and his dream of doing something truly adventurous was within reach. The adventure was a serious one though, and it required of him a level of skill and maturity that, in normal circumstances, took a lifetime to acquire. Being a team player by nature, he took very seriously the responsibility of flying six fellow crew members on dangerous missions night after night. By January 1944, the crew had 30 missions under their belt, and despite some nasty situations, their luck was holding.

Luck for Major Gordon Layzell, dropped into Albania by the Storey crew in November 1943, had not held. In early February, Lieutenant Colonel Norman Wheeler's party were occupying two houses in the mountainside village of Staravecka when the house in which Layzell had been staying suffered a chimney fire. Thinking that the house was on fire, he quickly gathered his kit and slung his machine gun over his shoulder. The gun went off. Marcus Lyon rushed into the room to find that Gordon Layzell had accidentally shot himself in the head. He was tended by Jack Dumoulin, but died in the early hours

---

[10] Let the Rest of the World go by. Music by Ernest R. Ball; lyrics by J. Keirn Brennan, M. Witmark & Sons publisher, 1919.

of the following morning. Tragedy enough, but there was more. The aircraft bringing in the supplies, Halifax BB444 of 624 Squadron, piloted by the newly-arrived Flight Sergeant Tennant, suffered engine failure while circling for the drop, lost height, and crashed into a mountain.[xvii] Flight Sergeant Baker in the rear turret was the only survivor, and by the time Wheeler and Lyon had made their way to the crash site, someone had already stolen his boots. The dead airmen, who had been operational for less than a week, were buried at the crash site and later reinterred in the Tirana Park Memorial Cemetery. Gordon Layzell was buried in the corner of a meadow close to the village of Staravecka and also reinterred in the Tirana Park Cemetery.[xviii]

From February onwards, it is noticeable from the records that the Storey crew went from flying almost exclusively in Halifax JN888 (Rita) to flying a variety of different aircraft. This may have been organisational as the Squadron now came under 334 Wing, but it is also likely that with a limited number of aircraft, pressure was put on the available crews to man whichever aircraft was serviceable for that night's operations. A typical crew's day, provided they had not been flying that night, would be to rise at 0700, have breakfast, maybe do a bit of laundry and then go to the flight office to see if your crew was down for an operation that night. Engineer Charlie Keen and Wireless Operator Walter Davis usually went out to the aircraft in the morning; Charlie to check everything with the efficient and friendly ground crew, and Walter to conduct his daily inspection, calling on the wireless mechanics if required. These ground crews worked miracles to keep the aircraft fit to fly. After the aircraft checks there would then be time to kill, with perhaps a game of cards, or letters to write home, lunch, and then to the briefing at 1600 to find out the target for that night. The pace would then quicken with flight plans to make, gear to collect and, finally, the walk out to the aircraft. Take-off would be around 1900 and, all being well, the crews would be back at the base between 0230 and 0400 the next morning. Debrief was at 0500, followed by breakfast of poached egg and bread and then the men went to bed, exhausted, at 0600. Another crew would be just waking up and would fly the same aircraft that night.

So it was not in JN888 'Rita', but Halifax BB381 that the Storey crew made their first flight to the northern Italian Alps, with supplies and four agents.[11] This was the first night that the Squadron were to operate on Italian targets and they were joined at the briefing by a number of Americans from 62 Squadron, who were about to start supply dropping themselves. The met forecast had given fair spells for northern Italy, but 'much vicious cloud to get through en-route'. Tom took off at 2020 and flew over the Adriatic at 2000ft. A couple of hours later he started to climb in order to cross the coast, but at 9000ft heavy icing forced him back down to 2000ft. He spotted a break in the cloud and began to climb again but found that icing made it impossible to get above 9000ft. All but two of the ten aircraft that had set out for Italian targets found similar conditions and returned to base with their loads. The crews were not yet familiar with the run up to the Italian Alps, which was tricky from a navigational point of view because of the long haul up the coast over water, and then, once over land, the mountain terrain generated dangerous up currents which threw the aircraft around violently and made the dropping grounds very difficult to spot. Only a small number of operations on Italian targets were successful in the first month, and bad weather hampered operations more generally, meaning many 'grounded' days for the Squadron.

Then news came through on the 24th February that they were to operate for the first time over Polish targets, and the

---

[11] ACOMB, VITAL and FUNNY (dropping grounds in northern Italy)

Patrick Stradling
(Photo courtesy of Stradling family)

competition amongst the crews, who all wanted to be selected for the job, was keen. One of the old Liberators, AL530, piloted by Flight Sergeant Horwood, was dug out of temporary retirement and six aircraft were fitted with overload tanks for the long round-trip to Poland. Eddie Elkington-Smith, 'pinpoint Elk', was aboard the Liberator as bomb aimer that night, and, although they reached their target, they were unable to see the ground, even from 2000ft. All the effort of that night – a round trip of ten hours – was for nothing, and Eddie hated the Liberator. "I don't know why but whenever the Liberator flew they plonked me in as bomb-aimer. I didn't like it. I hated the damn thing. No operation that I did in the Liberator was successful."[xix] In fact all the Polish and Balkan operations failed that night because of bad weather.

Twenty-three year old Air Gunner Patrick Stradling, from County Clare in Ireland, joined the Storey crew at the end of February, having flown 300 hours since joining 148 Squadron, most of it with Cyril Fortune. He would have continued flying with him except that Fortune had completed his tour of duty and was due some well-earned leave.[xx] So, at the end of February 1944, the final Storey crew of Tom, Hap, Eddie, Walter and Jim was joined by 'the last despatcher on Fortune's Coleen', Patrick Stradling.

CHAPTER 4

MARCH/APRIL 1944

The merciless winter conditions that had arrived over the Balkans in December, and persisted throughout January and February, continued to disrupt Squadron operations into early March. Things would improve in coming months, particularly once the American Dakotas began air-dropping operations, but weather and shortage of aircraft in the spring of 1944 made it difficult for the Squadron to maintain regular supply deliveries. Some areas had higher priority than others and signals from the field were getting tetchy; this from Basil Davidson's SAVANNA Mission in Yugoslavia: "Now two days since you advised delivery loads in reply to urgent call for support – STOP – Understand your difficulties but am relying on you to send loads on highest – REPEAT – highest priority", and, "Try show some understanding of workings here and not just keep sending excuses".[i] In northern Greece, the LAPWORTH Mission received no air drops for 115 days between February and June, and Head of Station Major McAdam[1] reported that they had been snowed-in for days on end during those harsh months and, despite preparing for reception of aircraft every night with 150 mules standing by, none came, and so eventually stores were ferried to them by mule over the mountains from the GEOFFREY Mission station.[ii]

---

[1] Major McAdam (previously Head of TINGEWICK Mission)

The Storey crew delivered one of those GEOFFREY loads in early March and the difficulties they had to overcome that night gives some idea of the problem, from both delivery and reception angles. They were in Halifax BB318, one of the older aircraft on the Squadron, their own being unserviceable, and the Daskhori dropping ground was in a deep valley. Tom thought his approach a bit too high and used full flaps to increase the rate of descent, bringing the aircraft down for a successful first run over the target. And then the unthinkable happened. Flying close to stall speed, wheels down and bomb doors open, the hydraulics failed and he couldn't raise the undercarriage, flaps, or close the bomb doors. The ground was looking awfully close. "Guide me!" Tom called out to the bomb aimer, and Eddie helped him to steer through the pitch-black valley; "Raise your port wing Tommy – there's a steeple coming up", while flight engineer Charlie Keen rushed to the emergency hand pump and gradually managed to restore hydraulic pressure.[iii] They gained height and climbed out of danger, but they still had supplies on board, and so returned to the valley where they found that the reception group, thinking the full load had been dropped, had put out the fires and gone. Mechanical failure at such a critical point forced the crew to confront their worst fears, but each had gained reassurance from the steadiness of his comrades and the dependable conduct of the skipper, whose insistence on procedure and discipline had paid dividends. Walking away from the plane that night, one of the crew turned to Walter, who had a dry sense of humour and never took offence at the jokes, and said: "So, God not quite ready for you yet, Walter?"

It had been a bad night for the crew, but for the Squadron as a whole, poor weather, mechanical failures and the loss of an aircraft had led the wing commander to declare it a "calamitous" one[2]. Only three of the twelve crews on operations that

---

[2] Taken from Squadron ORB Summary for 2nd March 1944

night were successful, and before these returning crews could land in the early hours, the runway had to be cleared of debris left behind by a Polish aircraft which had crashed on take-off.[iv] The worst news of all was that the Botham crew, in Halifax HR660, had failed to return from northern Italy, and although Spitfires from 1435 Squadron were scrambled to do a sea-search up the coast in case they had ditched, no trace was found. When news did begin to come in, it wasn't good. The aircraft had been hit by flak over Ancona and, with an engine on fire, Flight Lieutenant Botham had turned inland, reached his target, and then baled out the crew, leaving himself and Flying Officer Henry Lancaster, who was on his first operational flight, to stay with the aircraft to the end. Ten airmen had been on board that night; the crew of seven, plus three crew members fresh out from England who had joined the flight to gain operational experience as observers. Five of the crew perished and five survived, becoming prisoners of war.

The only encouraging news to come out of the night was that Flight Lieutenant Reynolds' Halifax JN896, which had been fitted with the new Rebecca/Eureka ground-to-air-radar system, managed to drop to the GEOFFREY Mission despite no signals having been seen. The Rebecca part of the system was the direction-finding equipment in the aircraft, and the Eureka part a portable ground-based beacon. Delighted with this first success, the Reynolds aircraft headed back to Greece the following night for another trial of the system, but this time the weather and severe icing forced them back early. Nevertheless, it had been shown to work, and this augured well for the success rate of future operations. There was little patience or understanding on the ground for the failure of supply operations over this bleak winter, though, to be fair, much of this was directed at those who ordered and prioritized the air drops rather than the crews themselves. John Mulgan, a British liaison officer with the KIRKSTONE Mission in Greece recalled this period in early 1944, when the men on the ground felt abandoned by those who had sent them into the field with inadequate support, but who nevertheless remained grateful to the crews who tried hard to deliver.

"One night a plane came overhead and circled trying to find us through the cloud, but mist thickened to rain and, finally, we could hear the plane flying away westward. Later, in March, a plane found us. The weather was still dirty with clouds blowing across the moon, but they saw our fires and came down, then lost them again before they could drop the stores. There were high peaks around there and the ground was dangerous. So we waited in the mist and wind, listening to the drone of the plane above the cloud and knowing that they would not leave if possible without finding us again. We waited there for a quarter of an hour hearing the noise of the engine coming close and then disappearing, and thinking each time that perhaps it had been unable to stay and had left, until finally, there was a brief rift in the clouds and out of them down on to the fires came this Halifax, like a friend, and dropped all its stores in two brief circles and then flashed its lamp in farewell. In better times and weather, later on, aeroplanes with stores were more commonplace. This first one was salvation. We knew that we could be all right after this for a month or so, and could stop feeling like forgotten men."[v]

It was the Edwards crew who had made that successful drop, stubbornly remaining over the target, a particularly hazardous one in mountain terrain, until a window in the clouds opened up and made a drop possible, but the perseverance and commitment of the Edwards crew was typical. The Storey crew had dropped at the same dropping ground back in December and encountered almost identical conditions of thick cloud right up to the target. Engineer Charlie Keen had taken an astrofix[3] two hours in to the flight, and they arrived over the dropping ground at Anatoli on time, but received no reply to the flashed letter of the day and so headed back to the coast to get an accurate pinpoint before returning to try again. This time their flashed signal was answered and, just as the cloud cover began to close in, they spotted the nine fires in a square, as briefed, and swept down through the mist to drop the supplies in three runs. As they roared off into the night, the cloud closed in leaving the area completely obscured once again. John Mulgan wrote his words about the Halifax: "arriving like a friend" in a handwritten memoir that he posted to his wife for safekeeping in March 1945. A clever, sensitive and decent man, he died in an Athens hotel room the following month from a deliberate overdose of morphine. Not all the casualties of war appeared on the official statistics; there were some, like John Mulgan, whose peace of mind was not restored when the struggle drew to a close.

Failure after failure continued to dog the northern-Italian operations, and the reasons were many and various. Aircraft encountered heavy fire from the ground while flying over occupied territory en-route and, when they got there, unpredictable air currents generated by the mountains rendered aircraft almost uncontrollable. A selection of comments from the Operations Record Book makes it clear what the difficulties were from the crew's point of view: "Unable to pinpoint because of cloud...Aircraft found to be off track impossible to define position", and, "Target very difficult and unsuitable for non-moon periods". In one case a group of personnel refused to jump when over the dropping ground. Wing Commander Pitt decided to interview a selection of pilots in an attempt to pin down the reasons for the poor results, and he found that, quite coincidentally, technical failures had

---

[3] Fixing their location using the stars, a common method of navigation on night flights

been higher than normal and pilots reported high numbers of "No reception at target". He sounded rather sceptical about the latter in his subsequent report, but lack of familiarity with the area was certainly a factor. Another was that Italy was more heavily German controlled than the Balkans, and it had been shown in Europe that this led to a high failure rate. The conclusions drawn at the end of the exercise were that better weather and moonlight were required for northern-Italian supply drops, and the obvious point was made that closer liaison should take place with the army as regards the selection of reception areas. The ABRAM dropping ground was an example of an unsuitable site, being in a deep valley and only visible when the aircraft was directly overhead. The wing commander concluded that "Insufficient thought was given to the flying limitations of a Halifax", when the army was planning drop zones.[vi]

The detailed planning for an operation began as soon as the crew had been briefed on their destination for the night. The navigator would assess likely wind direction and the pilot would determine, in advance, the direction for the safest run in to the drop zone, i.e. parallel to a hill or mountainside. Once over the dropping ground the pilot would then adjust his controls to counter the effects of crosswinds. The bomb aimer, waiting to hear from the navigator that they were over the target, would then have to take all these competing forces into consideration when timing the release of parachuted contain-ers, which could, in spite of meticulous planning and skill, still be carried off target by unexpected wind currents gener-ated by the terrain. Eddie Elkington-Smith, experienced bomb aimer on the Storey crew, ruefully recalls getting it wrong on a drop in the Italian Alps. The aircraft was being thrown around by dangerous up-currents, and in spite of a well-practiced procedure the containers drifted off-course and were last seen tumbling over the edge of an Alpine plateau.[vii] Two stand-down days in March 1944 were used by the Squadron to carry out delayed-drop tests from 3000ft, to see whether the bombsight could be used to allow both for the forward travel of the load before the chutes opened, and also for the drift of the chutes after opening. Being able to estimate the strength and direction of the lower winds seemed to be the critical factor, plus the fabric of the parachutes, which were prone to rip with the shock on exit. Until further tests were complete, it seemed that success still depended on the judgement and experience of pilot, navigator and bomb aimer, but the high failure rate and waste of supplies was prompting efforts to refine dropping techniques.

One route up to the Italian Alps took aircraft over German-occupied Rome, La Spezia and Genoa, and the crew were given an unusual exercise to perform on the way; they called it "Playing silly B's". As they flew past Rome they turned towards the city in mock attack and, as they did this, the city lights would go off, the searchlights and sirens would come on, and up would come the flak. They then turned back on course and did the same over La Spezia and Genoa, knowing that, half-an-hour behind them another aircraft would do the same, making sure nobody on the ground got any rest. The reason for these mock attacks puzzled me, particularly as the aircraft did not carry bombs and seemed to be presenting themselves as targets unnecessarily, but the mock bombing raids were part of a wider picture in the spring of 1944. Allied troops had landed on the Anzio beaches in January[4] and been unable to break out and move on Rome. During this period of stalemate Eisenhower and Montgomery had moved on to prepare for the invasion of France. It was given to General Wilson, Supreme Commander Mediterranean, to reduce the flow of supplies to German forces and make it impossible for them to move or operate effectively in

---

[4] Operation Shingle.

central Italy. He issued a memorandum stating that: "The main function of all classes of bomber aircraft in a land campaign is to interfere with the movement of enemy forces and their supplies". He was referring to traditional bombers, but the objective was to tie down the enemy, force them to expend ammunition and keep them away from the planned Overlord front and the Anzio beaches.[viii] Mock attacks by Halifax supply aircraft on a regular run up to Northern Italy were probably quite effective at assisting this strategy of disruption to enemy supply lines.

"Maximum effort on Polish targets" was the instruction from 334 Wing for the 16th March, and all ten available aircraft were fitted with overload tanks for the trip, but a poor met forecast in the early afternoon meant removing all the overload tanks – an enormous effort – and the aircraft were switched to Italian and Greek targets. The Storey crew were given a supply drop to resistance fighters near Susa in the Piedmont region of northern Italy,[5] and their recollections of that night would have nothing to do with the frustrating lack of reception signals in perfect visibility, but the sight of a huge glow in the sky as they turned for home. "The boys must have bombed Genoa and La Spezia," they said, but no, it wasn't that and as they flew on the glow got bigger. "Surely they haven't done Rome?" No, they could see that it wasn't Rome, and still the glow was getting bigger. "Good God, have the Germans bombed Naples?" They got closer and were finally able to see that the glow in the sky was coming from Vesuvius. It had erupted while they were airborne and was spewing out red-hot lava and sending smoke and flames high into the night sky. The crew had never seen anything like this before and decided to go in for a closer look, but an unexpected consequence of this action gave them a nasty shock.

---

[5] Dropping ground ACOMB

Hot debris melted on the aircraft's plexiglass windscreen and reduced visibility to zero, forcing the penitent crew to land that night with Tom hanging out of the side window to see where he was going. There was great relief all round when, on getting back, they found that the wing commander had arrived back with his aircraft in even worse condition. In a far more perilous situation were the crews of the 340th Bomb Group stationed at Pompeii Airfield just a few kilome-

Vesuvius, March 1944
(Photo from NARA in College Park, MD)
courtesy of Don Kaiser http://www.
warwingsart.com/12thAirForce/
Vesuvius.html Image 17:

tres from the foot of Mount Vesuvius. Almost all of their B-25 Mitchell medium bombers were damaged by the hot ash and some were even tipped onto their tails by the weight of debris.[ix] To have Vesuvius erupt at this critical period of the war seems almost theatrical – a force of nature exploding onto the scene as though the Gods had been unleashed in a fury. As the eruption progressed over the following nights, Brindisi itself was covered in a layer of volcanic dust.[x]

Fires and flames remained significant to Dad. In later years, he took enormous trouble rolling newspaper into coils for lighting a fire and then a double sheet would be stretched over the front to help the draw. We might be watching Top of the Pops, Mum busy in the kitchen, Cilla Black singing: "Anyone who had a heart would hold me...", and from Dad: "She can belt out a song that one!" Then, more often than not, the newspaper would catch light and the flames would shoot high – Vesuvius in our back room – momentary flurry of activity, smoke making us cough and then we would all return to our pursuits, Dad gradually retreating into another place, staring at the flames hour after hour, elbows rested on knees, bent forward watching the flickering and dancing curls of light, the murmur of our young, chattering voices barely reaching him. We didn't understand the significance of fires in those days – we were young and our minds were full of pop songs and school friends – but strangely enough it would be a fire that would one day lead us to an understanding of that "other place" and its significance for Tom. But that was for the future...

Spotting the fires meant that, for the crew, the long cold hours of flight had not been in vain and they could record a DCO (did complete operation) in their logbook. The reception groups lit them more in hope than expectation, as experience had taught them that, even if the planes arrived, they didn't necessarily drop. Basil Davidson of SAVANNA, after two months in the Vojvodina area with no supplies, put it like this:

> "Even when once or twice planes tried to reach us, we with the fires lit upon the ground could only hear the hum of their engines above the overcast, and they in the air could not see our fires. We would stand out in the snow for hours on end around a fire that Steve with inhuman skill had managed to kindle, lighting up at half past ten and tramping back to bed at two, wet and shivering, angry and disappointed. In the morning I would wireless: Planes heard over our fires zero one thirty hours. Confirm. And Base would confirm, trying to be cheerful: Sorry, no fires seen."[xi]

Mid-March was an unsettled period at Brindisi base: the Squadron was forced to make contingency plans for civil disturbance by anti-Badaglio elements in the town. Sten guns were made available at Headquarters and at the tented camp, and armed guards were placed on all aircraft, but despite the appearance on the streets of a few steel-helmeted loyalist guards, nothing developed. Things were however developing in eastern Yugoslavia, where German troops had been massing for the seventh offensive, determined to reoccupy the Sava and the plain of Semberija (Operation Wegweiser).[xii] Caught up in this was Major Basil Davidson, who sent an urgent message to Cairo: "Enemy in Racha yesterday – STOP – grateful any help you can give by speeding up sorties."[xiii] The request was for ammunition and Bren guns, and Cairo responded quickly with two aircraft; Halifax JP161 flown by Flight Sergeant Clackett, which took off just after midnight, and Tom Storey's JN888, which having returned from an Italian drop at 0300, was reloaded and back in the air later that day heading for the SAVANNA dropping ground at Brodac. Major Davidson and Tito's General Sava waited for the supplies with the enemy closing in. They had been moving between Yugoslav territory and Hungarian-annexed areas on the far side of the Sava River in an attempt to liaise with left-wing resistance groups there, but were now caught up in an enemy operation to clear out partisan divisions who were making a nuisance of themselves blowing up trains and causing disruption on the Zagreb to Belgrade supply route. As the Croatian Waffen SS Division moved in, Davidson was forced to move quickly over the Sava River to temporary safety, and it was from there that he had sent his urgent signal to Cairo HQ. Flying conditions were poor, and the Storey crew were not optimistic about finding the drop zone, but unexpectedly, and to great delight, they found a clear cloud window over the target and immediately spotted the signal fires below. As they swept down and dropped the supplies bang on the signal fires, the partisans could be seen collecting the containers and a relieved and happy Tom Storey said: "Let's do a beat up" [6]. He banked and brought the aircraft down low again over the camp and Eddie, from his position in the nose, looked down and watched as the slipstream caught the fires and scattered them to the four winds. The partisans flattened themselves on the ground and Tom dipped a wing before setting course for home and roaring off into the night.

The story of this supply drop was known in the family as "The burning of Tito's coat", and other crew members spoke or wrote of the same incident. In all our anecdotal accounts however, the emergency supply drop was for Tito himself, who sent a signal the following day: "RAF saved the day but burned my bloody coat!"[xiv] Walter Davis remembered that a replacement coat was dropped to Tito and, years later at a post-war reception at the Yugoslav Embassy, the story of the coat was still talked about. I have tried very hard to find the evidence to corroborate this story, willing it to be true because the crew were quite sure of it, and as children we loved to hear it, but however much I trawl through records and log entries, Tito was eighty or so miles away at his HQ in Drvar at the time of the emergency drop. The evidence has not borne out the story and, although I live in hope of turning up that message from Tito, for the moment I have to accept that, if anyone's coat was burned, it was probably that of Basil Davidson or General Sava. Davidson barely had time to gather in his supplies before the muffled thump of enemy mortar-fire forced him to move on, rushing a signal off to Cairo to make sure that further supplies were not dropped on the Brodac pinpoint: "Cancel RPT cancel pinpoint Brodac RPT Brodac. Enemy attacked at four hours GMT STOP pinpoint and signals tomorrow – sorry." He sent a new pinpoint the following day, which was also quickly cancelled and finally a third,

---

[6] Beat up - to fly very low over those who are watching in celebration, or to show off.

Mezgrazia, to which P/O Harding in Halifax BB422 dropped a further load on the night of 19/20th March.

A real morale-booster in mid-March was the return of Brotherton-Ratcliffe and his crew, who had been hiding out and living like partisans since early January. Tom had flown his first sortie with 'Brother Rat' and so when the opportunity arose due to a bad weather stand down, he and the rest of the Squadron went along to hear Brotherton-Ratcliffe give an account of his experiences, and hopefully pick up a few tips on survival and escape in case they should need it themselves. The focus of operations had now switched to Poland and with DC3s of American 267 Squadron arriving daily to fly sorties out of Brindisi to Balkan targets, 148 Squadron was preparing to assist 1586 Polish Squadron in supplying the Polish Home Army, 800 miles from Brindisi. Halifax JN888 'Rita', in which Tom had flown more than thirty missions, would not take part in the Polish drops; she needed an engine change and Wing Commander Pitt told Tom to fly her to the maintenance unit at Maison Blanche, Algeria. He added that since he thought the crew were all "barmy" he didn't want to see them for a week! On the way there they flew over an erupting Stromboli, their second live volcano, and arrived in Algeria in time for Tom to celebrate his 24th birthday. Ever resourceful, he managed to get them into a hotel for South African airmen, rather than the tented transit camp they were assigned to. Tom left the hotel daily to check for an aircraft that they could take back to Brindisi and on the 5th April he came rushing back to say that they had all been put on a charge for staying at the hotel without permission! Luckily, Halifax JN925 was ready to return to Brindisi with freight and in their haste to get away before the charge took effect, Walter left his identity tags behind in the hotel. His mother had replaced the original string with a gold chain and a medallion which he found uncomfortable at night and so he had taken them off and left them by the bed.

Back in Brindisi, they now flew whatever aircraft was available and the main thrust of air drops was to Poland. Polish pilots, many of whom had made their way out of Poland after the 1939 invasion and headed for England to join RAF Squadrons, began flying supplies into their homeland from England in 1941, but the long-distance flights and weather conditions meant heavy losses for relatively low tonnage of supplies. At the end of 1943 an all-Polish Squadron[7] arrived at Brindisi under the command of Squadron Leader Krol and, together with 148 Squadron (who joined them in February 1944), they began supply operations to the Polish Home Army,[8] a well-organised resistance force that took its orders from the London-based Polish government in exile. The Storey crew, along with seven other crews, were briefed for a Polish target on the 12th April, and with clear skies forecast everything augured well for the operation. Unfortunately during three take-off attempts the plane swung violently off the runway and Tom decided not to proceed,[xv] reporting the problem as magneto failure.[9] A couple of nights later the crew took off with a supply load of nine containers and twelve packages for Home Army troops in the far north-east of Poland, close to the Belarus border;[10] a round trip of eleven hours which they successfully completed.

In an effort to provide further help to the Polish Home Army, a bridging operation got underway in April to transfer political figures, couriers, and intelligence material by air between London and Poland, using Gibraltar and Brindisi as staging points. The movement of personnel had previously been done overland which took weeks, but now that the winter snows had cleared it was possible to prepare a safe landing site near Lublin. Dakota FD919 of 267 Squadron left Brindisi for the first stage

---

[7] 1586 Polish Squadron.
[8] Armia Krajowa (AK).
[9] Magneto is part of the engine ignition system.
[10] Dropping ground WYDRA

of Operation Wildhorn 1. The logistical difficulties of this operation were enormous, and Flight Lieutenant Harrod and his crew, who had nervously been standing by for a month, encountered poor weather, enemy flak, incorrect lights, and then had to land and take off again from a ploughed field airstrip.[xvi] Luckily all went to plan, and back at Brindisi a reception committee of RAF and Polish officers greeted the high-ranking General Tatar[11] and four of his staff as they stepped off the plane on the first stage of their journey to London. The VIP visitors spent three days at Brindisi and, before leaving, the General gathered the aircrews together and, with Squadron Leader Krol translating his words, thanked them for dropping arms and supplies to patriots in Poland. He was then flown to Gibraltar and on to London, where he joined Polish HQ and tried to muster support for an uprising in Poland.

The penultimate operation to Poland for the Storey crew was on the 16th April; a delivery of supplies to Polish Home Army forces south-east of Zwolen.[12] The supply load of six containers and nine packages was considerably smaller than would normally be carried for Balkan and Italian zones because of the extra weight of fuel, which was carried in overload tanks in the wing bomb bays. The round trip of around 1,800 miles was on the limit of a Halifax's reach and once airborne, the crew would endure ten or more hours of thunderous engine noise, intense cold and the very real danger of night-fighter attack. The rear gunner had the worst of it in his cramped turret, isolated but for the echoing voices of the other crew members over his headset, and always having to remain alert despite the numbing cold and tight confines. A couple of days later the Storey crew were back in the skies for the night of the 'Big push' on Poland, but this time they would not return; it would be the last flight of Halifax JP224.

---

[11] Also known by pseudonym 'Turski'.

[12] Dropping ground JARZAB

CHAPTER 5

SUNDAY 23rd APRIL 1944

At 1938 hours precisely, Halifax JP 224 roared down the avenue of flares at Brindisi, eight minutes behind the Bruce crew and followed at short intervals by the nine aircraft of 148 Squadron that were also flying to Poland that night.[1] Earlier, at the afternoon briefing, Tom Storey had learned that he and his crew were to take part in a big push to deliver supplies to the Polish Home Army, and that nineteen aircraft, eight of Polish 1586 Squadron and eleven of 148 Squadron, would be taking part. The Storey and Chalk crews, in the second and third take-off slots, were given a target in southern Poland[2] and were to drop their supply loads to the Polish Home Army 9th Infantry Regiment[i], just outside the village of Franciszkow. Hap drew out a course to the target on a Mercator plan[3], taking care to avoid known anti-aircraft batteries. Eddie then drew out the same plans on his air-to-ground maps, so that he knew the landmarks along the route. Both crews were flying aircraft from a new batch[4] that had recently arrived at the

---

[1] Adred, Boyes, McCall, Fairweather, Bettles, Reynolds, Chalk, Blynn & Brown crews.

[2] 901 (KLACZ)

[3] Mercator projection is the method by which the curved surface of the Earth has been drawn on a flat sheet of paper. The lines of latitude and longitude are all parallel so the navigator can draw a straight line to his destination and know the compass direction to continually take.

[4] JP220 and JP224 newly built by the London Aircraft Production Group.

base, and both would fail to complete the mission, though for different reasons.

Eddie sat alongside Tom for take-off and set the throttles to full power, while the crew, in their take-off positions on the floor and facing aft, braced themselves against the rear wing spar. The aircraft gathered speed and, as they lifted off the ground, Tom retracted the undercarriage and adjusted the throttles to climb, keeping half an eye out, as always, for a suitable area to belly land in case of engine failure. The aircraft bounced and heaved its way through the turbulent cloud layer, and, once they had levelled off on a dead set course for Poland, Tom adjusted the controls to fly 'hands off', and flipped the lever on the left side of his seat to engage George (the aircraft's gyro autopilot). His hand would never be far from this lever during the flight in case he needed to respond to equipment failure or take evasive action but for a brief moment, with the tension of take-off eased, Eddie lit two cigarettes – one for himself and one for Tom. It was part of a ritual they had. Then, disconnecting the intercom jack from his headset, Tom climbed out of his seat and moved through the aircraft to check on the crew and exchange a few reassuring gestures and hand signals. The deafening roar of the four Rolls Royce Merlin engines made any attempt at conversation futile, but a 'thumbs up', pointed finger, or a pat on the shoulder usually got the message across.[ii] The loneliest place on the aircraft was the rear turret, where gunner Jim Caradog Hughes would have no human contact for the next ten hours, and it would be up to the skipper to relieve his isolation and keep him involved via the crackling intercom. Patrick Stradling's first task was to sort and rearrange the load, grouping the packages around the hatch in such a way that he could push them out in as few runs as possible when the time came. They were still four hours flying time from the drop zone, but the skipper needed to know that he could jettison the load quickly if a problem developed. The pile of bundles and packages would be stacked almost to the roof in the narrow fuselage and the only way past for a crew member who needed the Elsan at the rear of the plane, was to scramble over the top in full kit.

Eddie remained alongside the skipper as they crossed the Adriatic and then, as they approached Yugoslavia, he went forward to his position in the nose to get the navigator an exact pinpoint when they crossed the coast. Hap was a good navigator and didn't need much correction but Eddie, from his prone position looking down at the ground, would call out whether they were to port, starboard, or dead on course – he was proud of his nickname, 'pinpoint elk', and assisted by map reading every inch of the way. From time to time, Charlie Keen, twenty years-of-age and the youngest of the crew, took an astrofix through the bubble roof of his engineer's position and Tom, while constantly searching the sky for other aircraft, also kept a lookout ahead for landmarks to assist in navigational fixes. He imposed strict discipline in the air and permitted no idle chat over the intercom, which was reserved for procedural matters. This protocol was strictly adhered to by the crew, who had been in enough tight scrapes to know that discipline in the air mattered. Night fighters had rarely been encountered during Balkan operations, but the flight-path to Poland exposed the solitary and fully-loaded aircraft to attack by enemy fighters based in Hungary and Romania[iii], and to German anti-aircraft batteries located around Budapest. Gunner Jim Hughes needed to be able to alert the skipper immediately if evasive action was required – they flew alone and without fighter escort, so the rear gunner was their first and only line of defence.

Weather worsened for all the crews once they were airborne and, although most of the aircraft ploughed on for hours through the difficult conditions, eventually, lack of visibility, icing on the aircraft, or excessive fuel consumption forced most of them to abandon the attempt. One-by-one, fifteen of the crews turned for home without dropping their supplies, among them the Chalk crew, who had reached the Slovakia-Poland border before turning back with heavy icing, and half their fuel load used up.[iv] As an added complication for the returning crews, they were unable to land back at Brindisi because of the strong crosswinds that had developed while they were airborne, and they were all diverted to Manduria, an American base east of Taranto. The Storey crew pressed on, their progress punctuated by intense bursts of squally rain that lashed the windscreen, and by dense cloud banks that threw the aircraft around and reduced visibility. The skies cleared briefly as they crossed the Danube, leaving Budapest on the starboard side and, once over the Carpathian Mountains, they descended from 13,000ft to 3,000ft in an attempt to get beneath the low cloud on the Polish plain.

At 2,000ft, Tom was forced to shut down the port inner engine. It was getting dangerously hot and the oil pressure was dropping. To reduce drag he feathered[5] the engine and then, over the intercom, Hap said: "Twenty minutes to drop zone skipper". Tom gave the routine instruction: "Switch to full tanks, engineer," which was normal procedure; all drops were done on full tanks. Charlie made his way back to the switch levers, which were located in mid fuselage by the rest position, and switched from tanks two and four to tanks one and three. Events from this point on were not routine; the aircraft was minutes away from disaster. Shortly after the tanks had been switched, and six minutes from the drop zone, Tom reported over the intercom that the port outer engine had suddenly cut dead. The Halifax was now only flying on its starboard

---

[5] Feathering the propeller in the event of an engine shutdown minimizes drag.

engines, making it extremely difficult to control both course and altitude.[6] To lighten the aircraft, Tom gave the order: "Jettison the load". The containers were released from the bomb bay and Walter Davis was asked to break radio watch and help Patrick Stradling (despatcher) to jettison the internal load. The last words he heard before unplugging his headset were the skipper asking the navigator: "What's the distance to the Russian Front?"[v] He sprinted back, taking his parachute pack with him, and helped the despatcher to push out the packages, but events were overtaking them. The aircraft was losing height fast and, struggling to hold a course, Tom tried to restart the port outer engine, and then the inner engine, but to no avail. He shouted: "Engineer, did you switch those tanks?" Charlie confirmed that he had, but was asked to go back and check. Realizing that he couldn't make it to the Russian Front, Tom turned the Halifax to the south-east, calculating that their best chance of finding partisans was in the southern forests. As they descended over the town of Rudnik, the roar of the engines caught the attention of partisan Commander Stanislaw Belzynski,[7] who was working late on the detailed plans for a raid on a German installation. He raced outside and watched the blacked-out aircraft pass like a shadow, low over the town. 'Had it been bombing rail lines? Was it trying to land?'[vi] Eight miles to the south-east in Sarzyna, Bronislaw Kaminski was enjoying a glass of milk at the kitchen table of a family friend, before setting off home to Tarnogora. Through the window he spotted the flickering red and green lights of an aircraft approaching from the west.[8] The lights seemed to come and go but, as it got closer, the aircraft turned south and then back to the north, getting lower all the time.

---

[6] See Appendix 1

[7] Code name 'Kret'.

[8] The aircraft should not have shown navigation lights, but it is possible that the switch, which was on the cockpit roof, was accidentally flipped during the on-board emergency.

Inside the crippled aircraft, they were at 900ft and Tom, unable to maintain height or hold the aircraft on course, gave the order: "ABANDON AIRCRAFT". The crew immediately stopped what they were doing and clamped on their 'chutes. Walter's calmly spoken: "Acknowledge – going out," were the final words heard over the intercom as they jumped into the night, one after the other – Walter, Patrick, Hap, Charlie and then Jim, who went separately in a backwards fall from his rear turret. Eddie paused briefly on his way back from the nose to see if the skipper needed anything. "Hurry up; I can't hold it any longer," said Tom, peering back into the darkness to make sure the crew were out – no intercom connection now. As the Halifax lost height, Tom stayed behind to destroy the aircraft's sensitive IFF equipment. "Woe betide the pilot who failed to ensure that this highly secret instrument did not fall into the hands of the enemy!"[9] Then he slammed the throttles through the gate for maximum power to the starboard engines, trimmed the aircraft to climb and scrambled back over the fuselage spars, slithering over the packages still strewn around the open hatch to make his exit at around 400ft.[vii] Baling out this close to the ground, he must have known there was a strong chance that his parachute would not open in time to slow his descent. 400ft is dangerously low for a parachute drop.

Heart thumping, he was immediately hit by the slipstream and pulled the 'D' ring at his chest to release the small pilot chute, which filled with air and pulled out the main chute. It was slow to open – seconds felt like minutes – and then he felt a sudden jolt and was swinging gently under a circular white dome. It was raining, and a Junkers 88[10] passed overhead as he drifted down. None of the crew had done a

---

[9] Words of Larry Toft, Halifax pilot.
[10] The Junkers JU 88 was a twin-engine, multi-role aircraft used by the Luftwaffe throughout World War II

parachute jump before and no amount of simulated exit procedure could prepare them for the shock of the real thing. It was dark, and Tom blinked the rain out of his eyes, straining to see if there were any trees in his path. Then bang, he was on the ground, stunned by a hard blow to his head, his legs twisted beneath him. He was aware of a momentary silence before his aircraft crashed to the ground with a dull roar, a sound also heard by Bronislaw Kaminski, the young man who had been watching the aircraft lights from the village of Sarzyna. He was now sure that the aircraft had crashed and rushed to share the news with the friends he had spent the evening with. They all set off for the clearing where they suspected the plane had come down, but then one of them suggested that the Germans might have prepared an ambush and they decided to leave it and go back in daylight. Kaminski walked home alone to Tarnogora where he met Jakub Pikula and Jan Mlynarski, who were on night watch in the village. He asked them where the plane had fallen and they said they thought it had come down in the forest.[viii]

Tom slowly came round. He felt dazed, his legs hurt and he stumbled about in the dark trying to release his chute and find somewhere to bury it. He was alone on a road and, as he

Wreckage of Halifax JP224
(Photo courtesy of Bibliotek Nowa Sarzyna)

staggered towards a nearby field, he fell into a deep, water-filled ditch and lost his grip on the parachute, which drifted away from him. His instinct was to go after it but he was too late – it was out of reach. He had come down between the junction of the San and Vistula rivers, on a main road to the east of Tarnogora village, from where a couple of dim lights were just visible beyond the stream and the field. His escape aids consisted of a compass and a silk map of Europe and Poland, screwed up like a handkerchief in his pocket. These items were of little use in the dark though, and his injuries made him very vulnerable unless he could find someone to help him. He pushed his life vest into the soft earth of the field and limped towards the houses in the distance, where he started knocking on doors. Nobody answered at the first darkened houses, so he crawled through a hedge towards a building with lights on, but spotted a sentry by the gate and realized it was a German barrack house. He backed away quickly. The next person he encountered was a young man of about seventeen, who stepped out of his house just as Tom was about to knock on the door, startling them both. Desperate not to cause a commotion, Tom gripped him by the throat to keep him quiet and whispered: "RAF, English", at which the young man, not knowing quite what to do, took him next door to the house of Jan Sowa who spoke German and might be able to help. German was widely spoken amongst the population and it was also a language that Tom had learned to speak well at Carlisle Grammar School[11]. He explained his situation to Mr Sowa, who understood and was sympathetic, but knew that, with German troops only a few doors away it would be impossible to keep him hidden for long. He told Tom he could stay for the night, and then sent his son, Bronislaw, to get help from Walenty Kida,[12] commander of the local partisan unit. Arriving

---

[11] Tom achieved a credit in German in 1936.

[12] Codename 'Klos'- Commander Nisko Circuit BCh - Bataliony Chlopskie (Peasant Battalion).

breathless at Kida's house, Bronislaw banged on the window to raise him: "There's an Englishman at father's house talking in German and he says he wants to be taken to the Partisans" he said. Kida returned to the house with Bronislaw and interviewed Tom, after which he decided to inform his superior, Zenon Wolcz[13], and then transfer the pilot to their hideout in the woods, a dugout managed by gamekeeper soldier Feliks Sitarz.

The soldiers of the Tarnogora German Barracks had, it transpired, been drinking heavily during the evening of the 23rd, and not only were they unaware of a British RAF pilot having crawled through their hedge just after midnight, but they appeared to turn a blind eye to the activity as Kida and Sowa went from house to house in the early hours, rounding up people to help smuggle the British pilot to the safety of the forest. Once assembled, they split into three groups and made for a familiar patch of woodland where, the previous year, they had excavated an underground bunker for the storage of ammunition and to be a staging post for escaped prisoners waiting to cross the River San. It was very dark and still drizzling and Tom, unable to keep up, was carried most of the way to the woods, where a system of signs and passwords got them past the sentries and to the camouflaged dugout beneath the forest floor. One of the men went down into the bunker and beckoned for Tom to follow, but he hesitated for a moment, unsure what they were going to do with him. Finally, after an exchange of hand signals and reassuring nods, he descended into the dugout and the partisans tried to explain, by way of hand signals and words in German and Polish, that they would be back later and that he should sleep. Leaving him with a guard and a single, lit candle, they withdrew, anxious to locate the crashed aircraft while they still had the

---

[13] Codename 'Wilk' – Commander BCh.

cover of darkness. As they left, they pulled the wooden lid over the bunker to conceal its whereabouts and to prevent Tom from climbing back out.

What a difference a few hours can make. He should have been landing in Italy with the other crews around now and yet here he was, alone, and hunched against the damp walls of a dugout for what was perhaps the loneliest night of his life. A thick fog developed in the early hours and Bronislaw Kaminski, who had been unable to sleep after getting home, was still awake when his mother got up to tend the cows. At first light, Leon Szuba called by the house with orders from Kida; Kaminski was to collect some food and take it to the forest where he would find an Englishman hiding in the bunker. The crash site itself had been alive with activity overnight as villagers and partisans tried to salvage useful material from the aircraft, which had plunged into a field between Tarnogora and the hamlet of Poreba, scattering wreckage across 200 metres. A Browning machine-gun and ammunition were retrieved by Tarnogora partisans, and another gun was taken away by villagers from nearby Sarzyna. Local farmer Sebastian Lyko found a revolver, a parachute and an airman's helmet,[14] which he took home to hide. Other useful parts, including a propeller and a wing section, were quickly taken away and hidden by villagers before first light, when the Gestapo arrived and began shooting to disperse them. It could have brought retribution on the village but the soldiers, who had been too drunk to take control of the situation overnight, were forced to cover for them, and so no immediate reprisals were taken. After inspecting the wreckage, the Germans realized that this had been a supply plane and, although they found bundles of leaflets scattered amongst the wreckage, they found no bodies. The aircrew must be in hiding close by.

---

[14] This helmet was presented to the Storey family by Piotr Galdys, in April, 2013.

A massive manhunt was set in motion, with reinforcements placed at checkpoints on the Krzeszow Bridge, the main crossing point over the river San, and on transport links further upriver at Bieliny and Ulanow. There was a lot of traffic in Tarnogora village that morning as Kaminski cycled to the forest with his parcel of food, and he noticed that the Germans, on foot and in cars, seemed very angry.

He found the English pilot lying in the bunker, one bare foot sticking out from the piece of cloth that covered him. Kaminski climbed down with the food and Tom raised his head and spoke to him in German. He said he wasn't hungry and didn't want to eat, so Kaminski ate some of the food himself; perhaps to show that it was safe, and eventually Tom was persuaded to eat a couple of the eggs that the young man's mother had cooked for him. By way of a thank you, he offered Kaminski a dry biscuit from his escape rations and then pulled a silk map out of his pocket and asked where

Bronislaw Smola, who was involved in the rescue of the airmen

he was. Kaminski was not sure whether he should tell him, so pretended not to understand the map. At this point, Kida, Sudol, Kusy and Smola, BCh Partisans from the village of Tarnogora, returned to the bunker, bringing with them some tins, which they believed contained meat. Tom took one look at the tins, which he recognized as having come from his aircraft, and said: "*Herr, es ist wasser*".[15] The men did not believe it until one of them pierced a tin with the tip of a bayonet and discovered that it was indeed water.

---

[15] It is water.

Tom once again took the map out of his pocket and asked where he was, and Kida finally gave the men permission to tell him. Kusy produced a red marker from his pocket and together the men looked at the map and marked an area close to the San River and said: "This is where you are". Tom put his hands on his head and his eyes filled up with tears. He took some money out of his pocket and tried to give it to Kaminski, who said: "No, you are far from home and you can buy something to eat with it". Tom's thoughts quickly turned to his crew; had they survived the descent and if so, where were they? Kida told him that German troops were out in force looking for them, but that his partisan unit had also sent out scouts and hoped to find them first. Some of the villages were in UPA[16] hands, which posed a danger for the downed airmen, and the old chemical works site in Sarzyna, which was now a German depot and surrounded by a high fence, posed another. The partisans were agreed that there would be no escape if they had come down inside that particular complex.

Kaminski had barely got home when Kida called by and asked him to return to the bunker and assist two people from the Kopki area, who were on their way to the bunker to talk to the English airman. Kaminski took Wiktor Galdys with him and they made their way back to the forest to guard the approach track and wait for the visitors. Kida had warned Kaminski to be on guard against Germans in disguise, and so when he saw a man and a woman walking towards him he shouted: "Hands up!" and approached them cautiously. The woman replied: "They've sent me here because of the Englishman in the bunker. I can speak English and I'm supposed to talk to him." Kaminski went to the bunker and brought Tom out to speak to them; a conversation in English that lasted about ten minutes. This, I believe, was Commander Zenon Wolcz, who had come to

---

[16] Ukrayinska Povstanska Armiya (Ukrainian Insurgent Army), an enemy of the People's Army of Poland.

explain to him that it was not safe to remain in the bunker and, as soon as it could be arranged, they would get him to the other side of the River San. Kaminski could not understand any of the conversation but noticed that Tom had tears in his eyes when the female interpreter spoke to him in English.

Engineer Charlie Keen was having an equally difficult time. His parachute descent had ended on a soft bank, which broke his fall but bounced him into a dyke, from which he emerged with a twisted ankle and no boots. This handicapped him from the start, but nevertheless, he set off down a forest track in his socks, mulling over possible escape options and coming to the conclusion that he could try to reach Tito's fighters in Yugoslavia. As he passed through a village, dark and quiet, his footfall prompted an outburst of dog barking, so he crept around the next one before arriving at a cluster of houses in the wood. He knocked on a window and frightened a young boy and his mother, who gestured to him to go away, so he kept on the move. At daybreak he met three German soldiers who were chatting to each other as they walked along on their way to breakfast, knife, fork and spoon in hand, and although his first instinct was to make a run for it, he decided to bluff it out and walked directly towards them in his khaki battledress and white roll-neck sweater. Remarkably, one of the soldiers stood aside to let him pass on the narrow track, and they continued on their way to breakfast, chatting and laughing. Charlie tried to get help at another cottage but nobody could understand him, though they did manage to warn him that the Germans were very close by – a fact that was becoming clear.

He watched from a hiding place in the bushes as truck after truck came along and unloaded troops, who went off to search the woods. He no longer felt safe on the track and went back into the woods himself, where he chanced on two young men carrying shotguns and decided to show himself in the hope that they were partisans. "English RAF," he kept repeating as he approached them, and to his great relief they were friendly and offered to get him some help. He asked if they could get him some boots and they said they would try, then they left him hidden in the woods. Two partisan officers, the Kumiegi brothers, were sent back to collect Charlie Keen, who had fallen fast asleep in some bushes. He vividly remembered waking up from a deep sleep to find two men standing over him with guns, demanding to know details of the aircraft and crew – nothing could be taken for granted in these desperate times. He showed them his identity tags and they wrote down the details and then asked where his parachute was buried so that they could retrieve it. Charlie could not remember and so the men walked him back, in the direction that he had just come from, to a lightly forested area where they were challenged by Kaminski, who recognized the Kumiegi brothers, but not the stranger –

"Hands up!" He said, and Charlie raised his hands. "He's English", said one of the brothers, but Kaminski was still worried that they were Germans in disguise and insisted that they search him thoroughly. Once satisfied, he led Charlie to the dugout where Tom greeted him with a surprised smile of recognition, followed by a sharp rebuke for trampling on his injured legs. The two men were delighted and relieved to be back together and, as they sat talking, Tom turned to Kaminski and said: "If we return to England, you can come with me and stay at my house – you will have everything you need and it will be good for you". Kaminski thanked him, but explained that his sister had been taken to Germany for forced labour and his

Bronislaw Kaminski, who witnessed the Halifax crash and assisted with the rescue (Photo courtesy of Pawel Cholewa)

brother had been taken by the Gestapo in 1940, so he couldn't leave his parents on their own.

That night, the first attempt was made to get the two men across the river. Battalion Liaison Officer Irena Wolcz[17], who was also the commander's wife, had spent the day making plans for the operation with partisans on the other side of the Krzeszow Bridge. At nightfall, she and her father visited the two men in the bunker, and, with touching kindness, took as a gift an English-style cake made especially for them. Tom spontaneously took the silk map handkerchief out of his pocket and gave it to her, saying: "You have been very kind and I would like to give you this."[18] Later that night Kida, Smola, Kusy and Kaminski collected the airmen from the bunker and took them downstream of the Krzeszow Bridge, where villagers from the other side of the river were to meet them with a boat to ferry them across. It poured with rain and they were soaked to the skin as they waited for the boat, but it didn't come. Then they heard shots and German voices coming from the road and abandoned the attempt. The partisans decided that the airmen were too wet and cold to spend the night in the bunker, with night time temperatures still dropping close to freezing, and so Feliks and Catherine Sitarz allowed them to sleep in their barn. A second attempt was made the following night, but with no signals received from the north bank, they returned once again to the bunker.

While Tom and Charlie had been trying to cross the San, it had been another eventful night in Tarnogora. The villagers were already complicit in the rescue and concealment of Storey and Keen, when news came in that two more airmen (Stradling and Hughes) had turned up very close to the crash site and were hiding in the home of Sebastian Lyko and his wife. The men

---

[17] Codename 'Grzes'.
[18] The silk map is still in the possession of the Wolcz family.

had landed separately and found each other by chance in the woods. In fact they joked later that it was a miracle they hadn't shot each other in the surprise encounter. Patrick had parachuted down next to a railway line and, despite landing heavily and hitting his head, he managed to push his chute into a drain and make for cover in a wood, where a couple of hours later he came across Jim who had landed on the other side of the railway line. They spent that day and night in the woods, sharing the contents of Jim's escape box and as dawn broke on the 25th, with reconnaissance aircraft overhead, they kept on the move under cover of the trees. Three hundred German soldiers from the garrison at Rudnik were now scouring the district with dogs, and a Fieseler Storch[19] spotter plane quartered the ground at tree-top height to try and flush them out. Fifty hostages were taken from a nearby village and the Gestapo threatened to send them to a concentration camp unless the villagers told them where the airmen were hiding. A German officer, who spotted four peasants dressed in khaki tilling the fields, thought he had found the missing airmen and immediately had them surrounded and taken for questioning. Back at his headquarters he gave them food and drink before discovering that they couldn't speak English, only Ukrainian, and was so disappointed to discover that they were not the airmen that he gave them a good beating before letting them go.[ix]

Stradling and Hughes walked all through the night of the 25[th,] and the next day saw some labourers working in the fields and decided to wait until dark and then approach them to ask for help. At nightfall they knocked on the door of farmer Sebastian Lyko, who took them in and gave them food while his wife kept lookout for the German patrols that were passing the house every thirty minutes. The isolated

---

[19] A single-engine short take-off and landing German Aircraft often used as a spotter plane.

farmhouse was very close to the guarded crash site and so, after they had eaten, Lyko hid the two men in his loft while his wife went to get help from Jakub Kak in the village. Jakub had been discussing the events of the day with Walenty Kida, and on hearing that two more airmen had been found, asked his son Michal to accompany Mrs Lyko back to the house and help to smuggle Stradling and Hughes into the forest. Michal was unfamiliar with the location of the bunker, so the group spent the night in the open, but at first light he went to Sitarz's forest lodge and found Smola who led them to it. Storey and Keen arrived back around midday after a second attempt to cross the San, and the four men greeted each other with surprise, laughter and relief.[x] Feliks Sitarz sent news to partisan headquarters that he now had four of the airmen at the bunker, but that lack of a common language was making communication difficult and Germans were already in that part of the forest looking for them.[xi] The partisans brought a damaged machine gun salvaged from the aircraft to the dugout in the hope that gunners Jim and Patrick would be able to get it working for them, but although they cleaned all the mud off and did their best with it, the barrel was bent and it was difficult to put the bullets inside the chamber. They eventually got it to fire a single shot, but only with the aid of a shoe!

Walter, Eddie and Hap did not make it to the dugout to be reunited with their comrades. Walter landed alone in a clump of trees and heard the noise of the plane as it crashed, praying that his friends had got out. He crawled towards an embankment, but heard a train coming and, realizing he was next to a railway line, he hid in a ditch as a goods train rattled past. He began to walk in a south-westerly direction, thinking that it would take him towards the Carpathian Mountains, but with no light to guide him, he stumbled into ditches, struggled through boggy ground, walked into barbed wire, and even heard whistles being blown, which made him think he had been discovered. He stayed on the move all night, despite the blisters from his floppy, leather flying boots, and the next morning found himself in open ground. To try and look less conspicuous, he smeared dirt over his sergeant's stripes and tucked his trousers into his flying boots. A spotter plane flew low over his head but ignored him, and by now he was beginning to encounter people and ask for help. He was treated kindly but with caution by everyone he met, but finally found shelter with a local woman. She bathed his bleeding feet, and kept him hidden until a local partisan officer arrived to take his details. It was here that he was visited by Private James Bloom of the East Kent Regiment, who had been captured by Germans at St. Valery in 1940 and sent to a Prisoner of War Camp in eastern Germany. He had escaped and moved east through Czechoslovakia into Poland, eventually swimming across the river San into Russian territory, where he was caught and imprisoned again – this time by the Russians. He now operated with local partisans under the name of Antoni Sawicki and he told Walter that he had no intention of ending up in Russian hands again. He said that as the Russians got close, he would walk through Czechoslovakia and make contact with the partisans in Yugoslavia. Walter, having just landed in enemy territory, could not have found this conversation reassuring, and his ordeal took a more frightening turn when some young men came and threatened to take him to the Germans and not to the partisans. Forty-eight hours later he was taken on a long journey by pony and cart through the forest to a safe house in the village of Rakszawa, and from there on to the home of Mr and Mrs Dec, in Smolarzyna village, where he found kindness and refuge. James 'Jimmy' Bloom, who had been in Poland for four years and spoke the language fluently, stayed in touch with him when he could, but operated with the local AK[20] unit, which was constantly on the move.[xii]

---

[20] Armia Krakowa (Polish Home Army).

Eddie and Hap were not so lucky and swiftly ended up in enemy hands. Hap landed in a muddy field, having lost one of his suede flying boots in the jump, and made his way to the nearest patch of woodland where he remained until dawn. At first light he realized he was on a track that was probably in use, so he hid further back in the bushes and watched as workers made their way along the trail to work in the fields. Later in the day he came out of hiding and showed himself to a workman who was making his way home, but was quickly told to get back under cover and wait, which he did. The man returned later with food and drink and told Hap to stay in hiding until nightfall, but Hap was worried that his proximity to the village would put them in danger, and when he heard barking dogs from the direction where his parachute was buried, he decided to move further into the woods. His freedom came to an abrupt end when he arrived at a high fence and, to the shock and surprise of both parties, he found that he was looking into the face of a German soldier on the other side of the wire. "The first German I had ever seen," he said later. He had accidentally stumbled upon the one place the partisans had feared, the old chemical plant at Sarzyna, which was now a major German munitions depot. From here he was marched along the wire at gunpoint to the guardhouse and then bundled into a car and taken away for questioning.

Eddie landed in a shallow pond and spent the night walking east, noticing as he went, a signpost that read Tarnogora – he could not have been far from the crash site. At daybreak he came to a wide stretch of water and was trying to work out a way of getting across when a local farmer arrived holding a plank of wood. Eddie took the opportunity to use the plank bridge himself and to strike up a conversation in the hope of getting some help. It seemed like a stroke of luck that the farmer had spent some time in America, spoke a little English, and seemed friendly, so Eddie went back to the farmhouse with him, was given some soup, and slept in the barn while the

Kopki Dwor, where Eddie was 'turned in'
(Photo taken 2013)

farmer went off to arrange his rescue. The farmer returned
with the news that he had found a man who could help, but
they would need to be careful on the way to his house because
German patrols were everywhere. Eddie was grateful, and
willingly followed him to a large manor house, Kopki Dwor,
where he waited, as instructed, behind a shed for the man who
was going to help him. The farmer walked away without a
backward glance and shortly after, a group of armed soldiers
appeared and took Eddie into custody. Kopki Dwor, once the
home of Count Tarnowski, was main German HQ for
the area, and Eddie, had been turned in by a Volksdeutsche
farmer.[21] He was taken off to a jail cell where he was stripped,
searched, and left alone. The next morning he found that Hap
was in the next cell, and they were taken together by train to
the interrogation Centre Dulag Luft, in Frankfurt, Germany.
They were treated well on the journey by their guards who
kept them hidden for fear of reprisals, and even bought them a
lager at the Berlin railway station where they changed trains.

---

[21] German settlers living beyond the borders of The Reich.

Once at their destination they went into solitary cells to await their interrogation.[xiii]

At Brindisi, a brief report in the Squadron record book read: "W/O Storey did not return from Poland and nothing at all was heard of him after take-off." In Ludlow, a knock at the door of the Unicorn Hotel in Corve Street with a telegram from the Air Ministry, told Rita that her husband of eight months was missing. In Sarzyna, the fifty hostages were released after the capture of Elkington-Smith and Congdon.

Chapter 6

RESCUED BY PARTISANS

A ll RAF crew were briefed on, and knew, the official evasion procedure: to conceal lifesaving equipment and move away from the crash site using woods and ditches for cover; lie low for three days; live off escape rations, and then seek help from isolated farmhouses or individuals. Tom and Charlie had been handicapped by injury and loss of boots, which forced them to seek help quickly, but their actions were in line with advice. This adherence to correct procedure together with a lot of luck had successfully delivered them into partisan hands. I say 'luck' because Eddie and Hap had also followed evasion procedure, and yet they were now prisoners of war. Walter came down very close to a forced labour camp, which is probably why he heard whistles, but he walked away from immediate danger and eventually got the opportunity to ask for partisan help, as did Patrick and Jim, who stuck closely to advice and eventually sought help from an outlying farmstead. It had only been a couple of weeks since Brotherton-Ratcliffe had given a talk to the men about his own successful evasion in enemy territory, which would have been fresh in their minds. However no amount of advice can adequately prepare a man for the trauma of being in an aircraft one minute, and on the ground in an alien landscape the next. The mental and physical strain of those first days on the run was acute, and it showed. Unshaven and in shock, Tom limping badly, they were a pathetic sight in their wet, mud-spattered battledress, but their youth and good manners aroused compassion in the people

Left to Right: Patrick, Tom, Jim and Charlie after baling out

·they met. The villagers of Tarnogora could not have been prepared for seven Allied airmen dropping from the skies into their midst, but this was a BCh stronghold, with a number of active partisan soldiers among the men of the village and, being a small, close-knit community, the network was in place to handle such an emergency.

Correct procedure now for the men was to place themselves unreservedly under the orders of the partisan commander, in this case, Zenon Wolcz, known as 'Wilk', head of the Nisko District BCh. It was a remarkable achievement for this unit to have rescued and concealed the men in an area crawling with soldiers and dogs, but two attempts to get them to partisan controlled forests on the other side of the River San had failed, and the Germans were closing in. They were trapped in a triangle created by the flow of the San River into the Vistula, which limited their escape routes and gave advantage to the

Germans, who could conduct their search in a contained area. The river presented a real barrier because all checkpoints across it had been reinforced as part of the search, and the dangerously fast current, generated by its course from the Carpathian Mountains, was a daunting natural obstacle. The stretch of river close to Krzeszow Bridge was too well guarded for another crossing attempt so, after liaising with an AK unit on the far side of the River San, Commander Wolcz arranged to take the airmen four miles downriver to a crossing point opposite Kamionka Dolna, where they would rendezvous with forty partisans from a specialist AK sabotage and diversion unit, who would help them to fight their way across if necessary.[i] The commander of this unit was Stanislaw Belzynski, a doctor of philosophy and university professor before the war, but now a partisan commander, totally committed to the resistance movement.

As darkness fell on the night of the 28th April, the four men, escorted by a group of BCh partisans, left the dugout and made their way through the forest to a prearranged rendezvous with the AK escort, who had brought an interpreter with them. The entire party then made their way cautiously to a natural curve in the river, opposite the village of Kamionka Dolna, and within sight of the German garrison at Kopki Dwor (where Eddie had been turned in). Had it been necessary to fight at this stage it would have been disastrous, as the pistols of the AK escort would have been no match for the machine guns of the German patrols. Luckily, they reached the river without incident. There was a large log lying on the riverbank which, when rolled over by one of the escort partisans, turned out to be a roughly-hewn-out boat; their 'ferry' to the other side. The men gathered to discuss how to manage the crossing, and it was decided that the party of twelve should split into two groups of six, with the airmen and an escort going in the first boat.[ii] The unstable, partially submerged boat was pushed away from the bank, and it rolled and swirled down the right bank of the river, over a sandbar and out into the fast-flowing current, with the men holding tight to their wounded skipper and clinging on for their lives. Charlie Keen, who couldn't swim, remembered it like this:

> "The current was fast and some of us slid into the water, but our brave escort, strong Polish partisans, swam alongside and caught us, hauling us to safety on the opposite bank."

As they tumbled from the boat they saw a young girl on horseback waiting for them and learned that she was to be their guide through the next section of treacherous marshland. Sixteen-year-old Nina,[1] the daughter of a hunting estate manager, had lived in these forests all her life, becoming a partisan scout and courier at the age of eleven, following the destruction of her family home by advancing German soldiers.

The River San looking towards the Krzeszow Bridge
(Taken in 2013)

---

[1] Aurelia Mierzwinska.

She made a lasting impression on the men as she moved unchallenged through the forests, speaking fluently in Polish, Russian and German, and they would see much of her in the coming weeks. On this occasion, though, after guiding them to safety, she said farewell and rode off to re-join her own unit.[2] After the war, Charlie Keen returned twice to Poland to try and trace her but, only knowing her nickname, 'Nina', had no success. Fifty years were to pass before the War Office revealed her real name, and Charlie managed to track her down, quite remarkably, to Southampton, England; just fifty miles from his own home in Brighton. They remained friends until the day he died.[iii]

Once on the other side of the river they came under the protection of a small, mobile forest unit[3] commanded by Jan Orzel Wysocki, known as 'Kmicic', and the final stage of their journey took them by car to the village of Ujscie, deep in parti-san-controlled woods, where the unit was based. Most of the fighters were away raiding a large German farm, but Jerzy Lyzwa (George), a recent recruit, was on patrol in the forest when a breathless young man came running up to him, saying: "I've been looking for you – there are two cars coming this way with uniformed men inside". George, assuming they were Germans, sent him to warn the village and then hid in bushes at the roadside to wait. The cars came into view, floundering through deep, sandy wheel ruts, and he noticed that the occu-pants were not in German uniform; the khaki was the wrong colour and they were not wearing hats. He then recognised the man sitting alongside the driver as Stanislaw Belzynski, commander of the AK sabotage and diversion unit, and felt confident enough to stand up and approach. Belzynski told him that the uniformed men were English, and that he was having difficulty understanding them so, as George spoke good

---

[2] AK U AK OP-33 unit, commanded by Joseph Gniewkowski ('Orsha').
[3] AK OP-33.

English, could he ask them some questions. Turning to the four bedraggled young men in the back of the car, George said: "Are you English?" To which they smiled with relief and confirmed that they were. Belzynski suggested that they continue the questioning at the village, and a runner was sent ahead to let people know that it was not the Germans approaching, but the English!

The car swept into the woodcutters yard at Ujscie under the gaze of a curious group of bystanders, and Tom was asked what they would like to do first. He replied, without hesitation, that they would like to wash and shave, if possible. He was too shy to admit that this was because they were not only very dirty and unshaven, but they had also picked up lice during their days of living rough and were desperate to get clean. George found them some soap and a razor and the woodcutter killed one of his chickens and set about preparing a meal for them.[iv] After they had eaten Tom lit a cigarette and the questioning began. Who were they? Where had they come from, and why? Tom introduced himself and his crew, one by one, and explained that three of his crew were missing, and he had no idea where they were. The gathered partisans then listened in awe as 'Tommy' described the sequence of events that had brought them to the Polish forest. For the most part he seems to have told them the truth but, either by way of adding a little colour or because of misunderstanding in the translation, the story conveyed to the partisans was that the aircraft had been attacked and hit by fighters over Czechoslovakia while on its way to supply the Polish Home Army, and although Jim Hughes had opened fire in defence, the crippled aircraft had crashed on Polish soil, forcing the crew to bale out. All faces turned towards Jim with growing admiration as Tom told them that he had shot down many German planes since joining the RAF. The partisans were impressed by the RAF men, and a bottle of vodka was produced.[v] Toasts were drunk to the brave partisans for having successfully pulled off such a daring rescue operation, and to the four young men who had flown all the way from Italy to bring them aid. Tom learned to say: 'Na zdrowie!' as he downed his vodka shots, much to the amusement of Smola, who had accompanied them all the way from the Tarnogora bunker. He joked later that these were the only Polish words Tom learned. It was just five days since they had baled out of their aircraft, and there was a huge sense of relief that they were out of immediate danger.

A couple of days later the men of the mobile forest unit[4] arrived back from their raid on the German farm with the bloodied body of a comrade, who had been shot and killed by guards. The mood became sombre as his closest partisan friends carried the young man's body to the crossroads at Momoty Gorne. There they dug him a grave with their bare hands.[vi] This was the reality of partisan life, and they would witness more harrowing events over the coming weeks. For the moment, the overriding priority for Kmicic (whose orders were to keep the RAF men safe) was to move them out of the village where they were attracting a lot of attention, and into the forest where he could keep them on the move. His unit comprised three officers and twenty men; among them a doctor, a solicitor, and several engineers, some of whom were on the run from the Gestapo after being caught in sabotage activity at the munitions factory in which they had been conscripted to work. Morale amongst these men was quite good; they had no choice but to hide in the forest and fight for their lives. The officers, however, were volunteers, and often accompanied by wives and families. They seemed to be more affected by the constant strain of the situation. Lieutenant Kmicic had set up this forest unit quite recently, but he was a veteran of many operations, including the raid on Bieliny Police Station that had provided his men with some of their weapons. Tom mentioned

---

[4] Armii Krakowa OP-33 unit.

during his debrief that Kmicic suffered from nervous strain and heart trouble, despite only being in his late twenties.[vii]

Partisan life was tough but there was a routine, a sense of purpose, and comradeship, which at times made it a good life. The airmen were accepted into the unit and treated as equals in every respect, except that they were not allowed to go out on raids. Instead, they undertook guard duty around the camp, and helped with the daily task of foraging for food. Being in safe hands themselves, they felt keenly the hardship and suffering they witnessed around them, which ranged from pathetic family groups burned out of their homes and living rough in the woods, to roaming bandits, who themselves plundered and robbed just to survive. The Kmicic unit had been attacked twice by Bolshevik bandits, as had local villagers, who complained bitterly about the theft of their livestock and carts. The Russian partisan units that were suspected of arming the bandits disclaimed all responsibility, and were engaged in a certain amount of plunder themselves. This forest, once home to a few woodsmen, was now a frightening place, populated by fugitives, displaced people, and resistance groups, including Russians and Ukrainians who, with the advance of the Eastern Front were filtering in behind the departing Germans. All were living off the land, their desperation fuelled by an awareness that they were slowly being surrounded by German troops, whose spotter planes flew over the forest from dawn to dusk. They might be queuing for their soup ration one minute and rushing for cover the next as a Fieseler Storch loomed over the canopy, machine-gunning the area. This danger was increasing daily as the encirclement of the partisan- controlled forest progressed. The daily physical and mental struggle took its toll on the men, but a certain amount of self-sufficiency was expected of them and they constructed their own beds, carried water from the river, and went out daily (disguised as woodsmen), in search of food. They called at local farms, where they could usually obtain eggs, potatoes and poor-quality black bread, but rarely meat, and whatever they came back with was shared equally. They often went without, but unlike some of the Russian and Ukrainian bands, they didn't steal their food, but paid for it with cash and protection. If they were staying in a farmhouse they would cook together in the kitchen, and then George would probably bring his guitar out and they would sing a few familiar songs together. In the forest, food was eaten cold, unless the commander considered it safe to light a fire. Alojzego Pajaka, known as 'Ali', who was assigned to Tom for communication in German, described the crew as young, friendly men who listened to everything intently and slept, ate and shared every task with the partisans, including the making of spruce shelters. Charlie Keen later commented: "They [the partisans] shared everything with us, and what's more, they thought of our comfort before their own. If it had not been for them, we would not be here."

Partisan activity during this period was predominantly to disrupt the German supply lines; blowing up trains and railway lines to harass the enemy as the Russians advanced and, in order to do this effectively, the partisan groups, AK, BCh and NOW[5], were in the process of joining forces. A week after the German farm raid, the Kmicic unit joined forces with one of the larger groups in order to intercept a train and free Polish prisoners who were being transported to a concentration camp, but, when they reached the planned interception point, it was swarming with German troops and a skirmish followed in which seven of the partisans were wounded. The injured men were brought back in carts and taken to a field hospital run by Father John's[6] well-equipped NOW unit, which specialised in diversion and sabotage operations and had in its ranks six Frenchmen who had escaped from forced labour

---

[5] National Military Organisation (Narodowa Organizacja Wojskowa).
[6] Franciszek Przsiezniak.

in Germany. The Kmicic and Father John groups were in the process of merging to form a single AK-NOW fighting unit in anticipation of the June offensive, and a degree of cooperation was already underway, to the extent that the airmen, who were left with a 'guarding' group during raids, were not always sure which of the bands they were with. Father John's unit of around 200 men and women was run with discipline and impressive military precision. Everyone was expected to attend morning and evening roll-call and daily prayers, reciting together: "Lord God Almighty, give us the strength and the power to persevere in the struggle for Poland..."

Every few days the Kmicic group would break camp at dawn and move under cover of darkness to a different location, sometimes staying in villages, but most of the time sleeping rough in the forest. The airmen were easy to pick out in the forest camp because they were dressed alike in RAF khaki, and always together. They remained polite and curious about every aspect of partisan life, and because they showed a particular interest in the weaponry, the partisans set up a target range with bottles to show them how to use the Mannlicher rifles (that they had acquired during the raid on Bieliny Police Station). There was a lot of laughter and leg-pulling, but all four men turned out to be good marksmen, which gave them great kudos within the group. The shooting contests became a regular sport and this, combined with a bit of slapstick humour and the singing of familiar songs, allowed them to forget the isolation of having no common language. Tom's German was quite fluent and Patrick Stradling knew a little Polish, which enabled them to get by, but they did not have the fluency to join in a conversation in Polish or understand what was being said around them, and they quickly learned that asking too many questions aroused suspicion. It amused the partisans that the men remained straight-faced when they were laughing at a joke, but on one memorable occasion, a partisan took out a small black comb and put it under his nose in an imitation of Hitler and sang a song, which had them all laughing. Some things didn't need words, and gradually a sense of kinship developed which would endure for a lifetime – trust, loyalty, humour and kindness were drawing them in to the Polish struggle for freedom. The fact that the airmen were able to beat all contenders in the shooting contests was certainly a factor in the developing mutual respect, to the extent that they were issued with the precious Mannlicher rifles when they were on guard-duty around the camp. They remained close as a crew, and kept their spirits up by singing familiar songs that reminded them of home – 'It's a long way to Tipperary' and, 'My Bonny Lies over the Ocean', and were soon learning some new ones. 'Kolysanka Lesna', a forest lullaby, was a very popular partisan song, and 'Moja Malgorzata', a love song that George sang when thinking of his wife, became a favourite with Tom, who was missing his own wife, Marguerita. They had married during his embarkation leave before flying to North Africa and he wondered how she was coping, waiting in Ludlow for news of him.

The gradual shift towards emotional solidarity with their comrades did not prevent the harsh physical conditions taking a toll and they suffered from cold, dysentery, infections and lice infestation. Tom's leg injury slowly healed, but he developed a painful foot infection, which was lanced with a knife and cleaned with the raw spirit usually reserved for drinking before a raid. He then succumbed to a bout of pneumonia and the partisans went to great trouble to get medicine for him. They had been living like this for a long time and had become inured to the hardship, developing expertise in primitive living and survival. They made poultices from beeswax and cleaned up their lousy clothing by stirring an anthill with a stick. They then threw the infested clothes on top for the ants to eat the lice, also leaving an acid residue to work as a natural disinfectant. The men strived to share every aspect of partisan life and would willingly have joined the fight, but in these early days, it is doubtful that they were sufficiently 'hardened' for guerrilla combat and they were not permitted to take part in raids. They had not entirely given up hope of finding a way back to the Squadron, and Tom asked AK Commander Belzynski if it would be possible to get a message to Brindisi to let them know that they were alive and in safe hands. Being familiar with the distances involved and lack of refuelling facilities, they probably had no expectation of a rescue mission, but simply wanted their families to be informed that they were alive. According to an account by Stanislaw Jankowski in his book, *Ostatni Lot Halifaxa*,[7] Belzynski did get a message to Brindisi early in May, but the response, when it came, gave no hope of rescue, because there were not enough hours of darkness for an aircraft from Italy or England to make the round-trip in safety and, even if an aircraft could have reached them, the required spec for a landing ground was impossible to achieve within miles of their current location. It was suggested that they try and make contact with a Russian partisan group, who might be in a better position to assist them. A couple of weeks later the whereabouts of these four crew members was reported in the Squadron operations record book:

> "Information was received today from the Polish ME48 that a message had been received by them from 'the field' in Poland stating that W/O Storey and three members of his crew are reported safe and in friendly hands. Further details to follow" *(ORB 148 Squadron Summary 17th May 1944)*

They had flown alone and were now lost to the outside world. Interestingly, at the same time, May 1944, SOE were making plans for a Dakota of 267 Squadron, fitted with eight additional fuel tanks and escorted by two Liberators, to take

---

[7] Last flight of the Halifax.

off from Brindisi and land at a prepared airstrip near Tarnow to drop off and collect key Polish personnel (Operation Wildhorn II), so it was logistically possible to mount such an operation to south-east Poland, but perhaps only in exceptional circumstances. Brindisi base, once the hub of their lives, was a receding memory for the RAF crew, who woke every morning to bird song, hunger and the murmur of Polish voices as comrades prepared for the day's raid, or went off to forage for food. They still wore the uniform battledress they had baled-out in, but their status as RAF aircrew, protected by the Geneva Convention, was compromised by their attachment to a partisan unit, and they knew that if caught, they would be treated as spies or terrorists and shot. Fortunately there were no ground attacks during this period, the forests being largely 'no go' areas for German troops, but it was a different matter in the skies, with reconnaissance planes flying over the treetops from dawn to dusk searching for partisans and machine gunning any likely groups they came upon. A new and worrying development was the dropping of signal flares by the Fieselers to guide in bombers for intensive and indiscriminate attacks, and it was distressing to see villages, where people had been kind and given them food, reduced to smouldering ruins, or subjected to murderous reprisal raids. Tom was particularly affected by the sight in one familiar village of men and women, victims of such a raid, hanging from the gables of their own houses. Something about this pathetic and pointless act of brutality not only tipped the men into wanting to avenge it, but haunted Tom for a long time. They toyed with the idea of forming their own guerrilla band, with supplies arranged through London – a sign of their growing anger at the unnecessary cruelty of the enemy and the solidarity they felt with their Polish friends.

The Germans were loathed for their cruelty, but partisans felt an even greater loathing towards the Russians, with whom they had been instructed, by their command, to cooperate.

They believed that in helping the Russians they were merely assisting a permanent Soviet occupation, but nevertheless obeyed orders and reluctantly escorted the Russians through enemy territory, and passed on information to them, receiving little in return despite the fact that the Russians received regular supply drops of arms and ammunition. A sense of national pride was a factor for the partisans who, though poorly equipped, were fighting on their home soil and were not prepared to take a subordinate position. The Russians, with their regular supply deliveries and disciplined militias, were scornful of their neighbours, and automatically assumed a superior status. They co-existed in a state of armed neutrality with neither side respecting or trusting the other, but the Polish scouts, whose information network was second to none, were bringing back reports of a massive build-up of German troops in the surrounding towns and now they needed each other.

The Polish units were poorly equipped for such a fight, and supply drops were a touchy subject because of the disappointment felt over the flow of arms reaching them from the Allies, for which they blamed Britain. Tom did his best to explain the difficulties of supplying them from such a distance given the prevailing weather conditions, but the partisans resolutely believed that their overwhelming struggle could have been better supported, had the will been there. A happier subject was the progress of the war, and they were particularly eager to hear news of the Polish units, led by General Anders, who were fighting with the Western Allies in Italy, and on the point of a breakthrough at Monte Cassino. They were naively convinced that Churchill was delaying the invasion of France[8] in order to preserve his forces to fight the Soviet Union over the Polish question, and they followed events keenly. The Polish underground newspapers, which were in wide circulation, and Polish

---

[8] Operation Overlord.

broadcasts from London kept them well informed, and both officers and men had been 'filled with despair' to learn of Churchill's speech to the Commons in February, in which he praised his ally Stalin and said:

> "Here I may remind the House that we ourselves have never in the past guaranteed, on behalf of His Majesty's Government, any particular frontier line to Poland. We did not approve of the Polish occupation of Vilnia in 1920. The British view in 1919 stands expressed in the so-called Curzon line, which attempted to deal, at any rate partially, with the problem. I have always held the opinion that all questions of territorial settlement and readjustment should stand over until the end of the war, and that the victorious powers should then arrive at formal and final agreements governing the articulation of Europe as a whole." [Hansard]

As cooperation between the Polish and Russian groups progressed, Tom saw an opportunity to follow up on the possibility of an escape route via Russia, and he asked Kmicic to take him to the three Soviet commanders in the area, Yakovlev, Nadelin and Kunicki, in the hope that they could secure an agreement to repatriate the crew. This was disappointing for Kmicic, who considered the Russians almost as much the enemy as the Germans and he tried hard to talk Tom out of it, but the discipline and leadership that had been Tom's trademark in the air kicked-in now, and he resolutely pressed Kmicic to take him to visit the Russian commanders.

While a glimmer of hope was opening up for Tom's group, Walter Davis remained hidden in the home of Jakub Dec, and was in the process of being given a new identity. The local AK partisans arranged false papers for him in the name of Wtadystaw Dec, and with this identity, and clothes given to him by the family, he settled in and began to learn the language.

There was no possibility of escape at this stage and Walter's fate was entirely in the hands of this remarkable family, who taught him Polish songs and jokes and treated him as a son. It is hard to imagine why they would put their own lives in such danger for the sake of a stranger, but this is exactly what they did, and the kindly Mrs Dec became a mother to Walter. The Germans were everywhere, but the family usually received a warning when they were coming and Walter was able to run off into the forest and hide until the coast was clear. A couple of times he didn't have time to escape, and the fearless Mrs Dec, who he called 'Matka', hid him under piles of bean plants in the loft, or out amongst the raspberry canes. Walter initially slept in a loft over the cowshed, but later was moved to a more secure hiding place inside a covered haystack, which was accessed by removable planks in a partition separating the haystack from the threshing floor. Gaps in the planking gave him enough air to breathe and, on one memorable occasion, allowed him to watch a group of German soldiers as they helped themselves to one of the Dec family cows.[viii] This would be Walter's life for the next five months, constantly in fear of being discovered and the consequences of that for the family who had been so good to him. Like his crewmates, he was no longer an RAF sergeant in the eyes of the enemy, but a guerrilla fighter, and he could expect no mercy if he were caught.

Walter Davis (centre) with AK Partisans
(Photo courtesy of Davis family)

Eddie and Hap spent their first five days at Dulag Luft in solitary confinement on a diet of bread and water, and were threatened throughout their period of interrogation.[ix] This was the main reception and interrogation centre for newly captured airmen, and a transit camp, the sole function of which was to gather intelligence before moving them on to a prison camp for airmen. The name is short for *Durchgangslager der Luftwaffe* (Air Force transit camp) and conditions in the wooden cell blocks were solitary and grim, with a bed and just enough space to pace up and down. A radiator tended to swing from very hot to very cold to make life as uncomfortable as possible, and a string pull in the cell was the only way to get the attention of a guard for a toilet visit. Eddie recalled two interrogations in the first few days, and he was astonished at the detailed information held by his interrogators, who conversed with him in fluent English, some having studied in England. They knew the code letters of all aircraft, the Squadrons to which they belonged and, in the case of Halifax JP224, they told him that they knew the destination of the supplies because of maps they had found in the wreckage of the aircraft. The interrogation techniques were sophisticated, and relied on the use of detailed and personal information to induce the airman to talk by convincing them that the Germans had the information anyway. Eddie was stunned by one piece of information the interrogators had, which related to an incident with Squadron Leader Brotherton-Ratcliffe, who had taken a Dakota into Greece to pick up personnel and, though he did return safely, he had spent a couple of days bogged down in soft ground. The interrogator dropped this piece of information into the conversation, saying: "We know all about 'Brother Rat' – next time he lands on our side, we'll have him". They also tried to pin sabotage on Eddie and Hap, owing to the load being jettisoned prior to baling out[x], but they stuck to a repetition of name, rank, and number, and were eventually released into the compound with the other POWs. One further interrogation followed on the 5th May, after which they learned they would be moved on to Stalag Luft 6, at Heyderkrug, in East Prussia.[xi] They were on the move again and, although I can only guess at how they felt, a few lines written by an unknown airman on a cell wall at Dulag Luft may offer an insight:

> "It's easy to be nice boys
> When everything's ok
> It's easy to be cheerful
> When you're having things your way
> But can you hold your head up
> And take it on the chin
> When your heart is breaking
> And you feel like giving in?"[xii]

CHAPTER 7

WITH RUSSIAN PARTISANS

Mikolaj 'Mucha' Kunicki and his Soviet partisan unit crossed the River Bug in the middle of April 1944, having received orders from General Strokacz, commander-in-chief of the Ukrainian partisan movement, to move into occupied Poland and disrupt the supply lines of retreating German forces. Kunicki and his battle-hardened unit arrived at Momoty Gorne on the 9th May, and Kmicic immediately invited him to his camp to discuss areas for cooperation, and to ask for assistance with the evacuation of the British airmen. Kunicki, who had just received an air-drop of supplies, was weary from his long trek and unfamiliar with the forest trails, so he asked Kmicic to come to him instead. Accordingly, Nina guided Kmicic and his party of twelve to the makeshift Soviet unit HQ, where they were stunned by the display of parachutes, radios, and arms scattered in abundance around the room. Moscow had even included vodka and wine in the supplies as a present.[i] Kunicki welcomed them and, noticing four unusually quiet, awkward-looking men in the group, asked who they were. "They are the English airmen", said Kmicic, to which Kunicki responded, with a mocking nod towards the old Mannlicher rifles they carried, saying: "Such weapons are for fighting the Germans?"[ii] This was not a good start, but the two leaders retired for private talks and discovered that they got on rather well. When Kmicic raised the subject of the airmen, Kunicki agreed to inform his command in Kiev of their request to be flown to Moscow. Once the formal talks were over a bottle of vodka was brought out for toasts, but Tom and his crew, uneasy in this new environment, did not join in. Kunicki found this difficult to understand and asked: "Why such long faces, and why do you not drink?" The crew shrugged their shoulders and remained silent.[iii] They were strangers among a group of people they had no reason to trust, and in this new situation they confronted danger as a disciplined crew, as they had throughout their Squadron operations. Kunicki cut a striking figure in his military trench coat and Russian Cossack hat, and George, who had accompanied them to the Soviet camp, described him as an energetic and decisive leader. He was Polish by birth and had seen service in the Polish, German, and Russian armies. Tom later described him as: "A fine specimen of a man"[1] and came to both admire and trust him, but at this first meeting, he was cautious.

The following day Kunicki's wireless operator, seventeen-year-old Ducia, tapped out a signal to General Strokacz, which read:

"In the Vistula region an English plane was shot down by the Germans. The crew of the plane, officers WARRANT, STOREY T and Sergeants HUGHES, FLICTT [?] and KEEN are with me and have asked to be sent to Moscow. Your decision?"[2]

General Strokacz, and First Secretary of the Ukrainian Central Committee Nikita Kruschev, could not have been entirely surprised by the news, since they were already aware of some unusual activity in the region south-east of Lublin. They had

---

[1] Storey debrief to Brigadier Hill (ANNEX II) 15th June 1944 (CAB 66/53/47) TNA
[2] Translation of a document found in Russian Archives (courtesy of Paul Lashmar)

been informed by Commander Shangin[3], who had recently entered Poland with a Ukrainian unit, that while waiting for a supply drop from a Soviet plane, parachuted containers had dropped from an unidentified plane, thought to be British. The unexpected bounty had consisted of German machine guns, ammunition, anti-tank rockets, grenades, and radios (with instructions in Polish). This was probably the jettisoned load from Halifax JP224. Strokacz and the Soviet Leadership in general, were particularly nervous about the infiltration of their units by German spies and, while it was likely was that these were genuine Allied airmen, it was essential to establish their identity before any decision could be taken about their rescue. Kunicki received a test question for Tom to answer on behalf of the crew: "Who is your Squadron intelligence officer?" To which he replied: "Curly Brown". A second question followed: "Why?" Tom answered, without hesitation: "Because he's bald". This information was confirmed as correct, though not through the obvious channel of the British Military Mission in Moscow, but directly through the Soviet Military Mission in London, which checked it with the Air Ministry.[iv] General Montagu Burrows, head of the British Military Mission, was kept completely in the dark about the stranded airmen, and would later respond indignantly to this slight.

Knowing the whereabouts of the men was one thing, getting them back was quite another. Allied servicemen were on the run or in hiding throughout Europe and the Balkans and, although escape lines were established in some countries, this was not the case for Poland, where the practical difficulties of flying servicemen back from such a distant location were compounded by Russia's refusal to allow Allied aircraft to land on Soviet soil. There could be no reasonable expectation of a rescue mission, and yet, in exceptional circumstances, it was

---

[3] B. G. Shangin, commander of a Ukrainian partisan unit.

possible, as demonstrated by operation Wildhorn II.[4] This highly secret bridging operation was executed by SOE Italy[v] without the knowledge of either the Russians or the Polish Section of SOE in London, and so there was little possibility of expanding it into a rescue flight for four NCOs, who were in the safekeeping of a Russian unit. The obvious escape route was through Russia. It was technically easier for a Soviet aircraft to undertake the rescue, but the dangers were still formidable.

I find it a mystery why Strokacz and Kruschev should trouble themselves with four British airmen, but they did agree to help, and a plan developed that involved Soviet ace pilot Vladimir Pavlov in one of the most dangerous assignments of his career. Strokacz informed Kunicki of the decision to send an aircraft to pick the men up, and instructed him to find and prepare a suitable landing strip, the specification for which was quite precise. It had to be 1,750 metres long with a turning circle at the end, and firm enough to take the weight of a 13-tonne aircraft. He went on to suggest that Tom Storey, being a pilot himself, should lead the search for a suitable field. Kruschev then sent a message to inform Stalin that a British crew were sheltering with a Soviet partisan unit, and that a decision had been taken by the Ukrainian command to mount a rescue operation:

> "We have given KUNITSKY urgent instructions to select a landing strip. As soon as the strip is ready, we will immediately transfer the English airmen to Kiev. We have suggested to SHANGIN that he should forward the instructions and orders in Polish to the Central Committee of the Ukrainian Communist Party at the first opportunity."[vi]

---

[4] Bridging operation using a Dakota of 267 Squadron to take Polish political, military and intelligence personnel in and out of Poland to England, via Brindisi.

On the 24th May, Kunicki gathered the men together to read out a telegram he had received from General Strokacz, letting them know that their families had been informed that they were in safe hands.[vii] Rita received her telegram at the Unicorn Hotel the following day, the 25th May, and the Stradling family in Ireland received theirs at the beginning of June. It puzzles me that Belzynski seems to have got an 'in safe hands' message through to Brindisi at the beginning of May, which the Squadron reported in their record book on the 17th May, and yet the families were not informed until the confirmation of their identities via Strokacz. Was it to protect the three airmen whose whereabouts were not known, or to spare the families from receiving good news that might later turn out to be false?

General Strokacz ordered Kunicki, in that same telegram of the 24th May, to keep the airmen out of danger, and Kunicki took his orders seriously. Tom was genuinely grateful for this

Left to Right: Keen, Kunicki, Hughes, Storey, Ducia, Stradling

protection, but when asked the inevitable question about the purpose and destination of his flight over Poland, he did not give a truthful account, but instead gave one that was likely to impress. The secret nature of their work had been so drummed-in to the crews that Tom did not reveal the complete nature of the flight to anyone, though he came closest when talking to the partisans of the AK forest unit, who already knew about the supply flights from Italy. He seems to have adjusted his story according to the level of trust he felt, and he told Kunicki the same fanciful story he had come up with for the NOW partisans of Father John's unit[viii] – that his Squadron had been ordered to bomb the oil wells at Drohobych[5], and while over Poland his aircraft had been attacked and damaged by eight Messerschmitt. He claimed to have shot down three of the enemy aircraft before receiving a hit in one of his engines, and then a second engine failed, which forced him to jettison the bomb load. He said he had tried to reach the Soviet lines between Kovel and Lvov, but had to order the crew to bale out when a third engine started to fail, finally jumping himself. He stuck to this fictional account, which had just enough truthful information to be plausible though it would not have fooled anyone with knowledge of the firepower of a special duty Halifax. Kunicki, dubious though he may have been about this colourful account, would certainly have liked the idea of Allied planes bombing the Drohobych oil wells, being under orders himself to destroy similar installations. Strokacz, having received Shangin's report, knew that the aircraft had been on a supply mission, and this was the information he passed on to Stalin.

The airmen began to settle into the routine of the Russian camp with renewed hope of rescue, and were reassured by the

---

[5] Drohobych oil fields south of Lvov, formerly part of Poland, then annexed to Russia during German-Soviet pact, and latterly in German hands after Barbarossa.

knowledge that Kmicic, who had been reluctant to hand them over, had set up his camp a short distance away in order to keep an eye on them. They struggled to understand or be understood by this comradely band of Uzbeks, Russians, Tatars, Ukrainians and Hungarian Jews, though George remained with them and did his best to interpret and Tom could talk to Kunicki in German so that orders were understood and obeyed. Because of Strokacz' order to keep the men safe, Kunicki made sure that they were always with him and, since he rarely moved without Ducia and the portable wireless set that was strapped to her back, they formed a tight group of six. Kunicki had around two hundred partisans in his unit, many of whom had escaped from German prisons or forced labour camps, and their ranks were augmented by officers sent directly from Russia. One of these was the political commissar, who was responsible for the education of the unit on behalf of the Communist Party, holding weekly lectures on the subject of Party ideology and principles. He also appeared to be keeping a sharp eye on the new arrivals, and took every opportunity to engage them in conversation about their activities in Poland. The female partisans, about twenty five in number, served mostly as cooks or wireless operators, and were treated exactly the same as the men, even sleeping in the commander's tent, but the British boys were not used to women soldiers and found them rather formidable, later recalling: "They were vicious – real partisans!"[6] Seventeen-year-old Ducia wore a uniform and was treated as an officer, rarely leaving Kunicki's side, but she would not reach her eighteenth birthday. Her lifespan could be measured in weeks, not months, and her death was certainly that of a 'real partisan'. Injured in the battle for Porytowe Hill on the 14th June 1944, she shot herself rather than be captured.

---

[6] Comment made by Charlie Keen, recorded in 2003

Tom and Kunicki left the camp on horseback every day to search for a suitable area to prepare as a landing strip for a Dakota. They needed firm ground or a stubble field that could be cleared and flattened, and which could be defended during the period the aircraft was on the ground; a tall order in this boggy, forested terrain, and several times when they found a suitable strip they had to abandon it when German troops moved too close for safety. Kunicki was philosophical about the search. If they found suitable ground, all well and good, if not, then he had four extra partisans for his unit. Tom's main recollection of these daily treks was the awkward horse he was given to ride, which rubbed up against every tree and gatepost it could find in an effort to dismount him. The horse had been given to the unit by a farmer, who had been unable to control it, and nobody in the unit had managed to ride it until Patrick Stradling asked to be allowed to try. Kunicki was reluctant at first, mindful of his orders to keep the men safe, but eventually agreed and Patrick jumped on the horse and fought with it until it became calm, at which point he dismounted and gave the reins to Kunicki saying: "Now it will listen".

The everyday routine for the unit involved foraging for food, outpost duties, raids on local towns, and the relentless sabotage of rail links, so that there were never more than fifty men in the camp at any one time. The blowing up of trains was the main military focus during May 1944, and the unit chalked up ninety-eight hits by the time the airmen left them. An attack on a train would be launched on receipt of a radio message, and the unit would set off to intercept either a troop or a supply train, sometimes using stick dynamite on the track (which partisans would detonate as the engine went over it), and sometimes laying a landmine on the track (which detonated with the weight of the engine). If it was a supply train they stayed to retrieve whatever stores or equipment they could from the wreckage, but if it was a troop train they disappeared very quickly back into the woods.[ix] The airmen were still not allowed to take an active part in the raids, but witnessed at least one train being blown up and were issued with Russian tommy guns and given 'alarm' posts.

When not attacking trains, partisan groups were often away foraging, scouting, or raiding local towns, but when Kunicki moved, so did the airmen, with orders and instructions given to Tom in German. One particular day they were on the move with a one-hundred strong contingent of partisans when they came face-to-face with an equal number of bandits coming from the other direction. Like a scene from an old western, they met on the dusty main street of a village, and not a single safety catch was in place on their guns, but it was not in either group's interests to get involved in a fight, and they passed each other in silence on the otherwise empty street. On another occasion they were spotted passing through a village, and information was passed to the Germans who sent in a Junkers 87 to bomb it flat. This was a pointless act because the partisan group was long-gone by the time the bombers arrived, and they watched from the safety of a nearby wood, consumed by anger as the bombs fell on yet another defenceless village. The next morning they walked back to find nothing but a pile of smouldering timbers. The long-suffering villagers not only lived in fear of such attacks, but constantly had their food and livestock plundered by just about every group in the district. The Soviet units were well equipped in most respects, but they received no food in their supply drops and so bought, stole, or requisitioned supplies from the towns and farms of the district. Kunicki, being polish himself, was sensitive to the plight of the local population and, unlike many of the Soviet and Ukrainian units, retained their goodwill by paying either in cash or kind for produce, and reporting back to Kiev incidents of serious abuse by other units. Two vital items that did not tumble out of a Soviet Dakota were vodka and a tobacco called 'Machorka', which was usually rolled and smoked in the 'educational' papers distributed by the political commissar. Most raids carried out locally were to obtain vodka, and it was seized in huge quantities – 80,000 litres in one raid alone, but the airmen were wary of the Russian drinking sessions. It was strong stuff, and they couldn't risk their tongues being loosened by alcohol, so it became necessary to stick together and make sure that no one was left alone with the political commissar, with whom they felt very uneasy.

Kunicki issued the men with clean underwear, equipped them with automatic weapons and allowed Tom to write a daily diary. They were given permission to have their boots repaired by the unit's shoemaker, and because of a lack of bedding, were issued with an old Russian parachute to cover themselves at night.[x] Most aspects of partisan life were harsh, but the airmen were finding that it could feel good to share the hardship with such worthy comrades, and despite the ever-present language barrier, friendships developed though music – a pastime they all enjoyed. George sang and played the guitar, and spirits were always raised by the mixture of homespun British songs and the catchy, sometimes mournful, Russian folk songs popular in the camp. Kunicki told Tom that he often had to send his men on suicide missions, and, with orders coming directly from Russia, there was never any thought of disobeying. The lives of the airmen seemed to have enough value for them to be protected, but it was not so for their partisan comrades, whose lives were held cheap and for whom the life-and-death struggle was to get much harder in the coming weeks. Kunicki was scornful of Father John, commander of the NOW unit with whom he cooperated, for issuing his men with leave passes to visit their families, finding this incomprehensible in wartime. The men of his own unit, detached from home and family and exposed to a great deal of cruelty and death, were somewhat brutalised by the experience and meted out savage revenge on any Germans they captured. Tom described the way prisoners were treated:

> "Prisoners were stripped to their underclothes and then shot. German spies, of which there were many, were

taken by horse and cart to the neighbourhood of the nearest German garrison, where they were split open and filled with straw or eggs. The horse was then whipped up and the still-living man was carried into the garrison."[xi]

Such acts always prompted savage reprisals, but the Polish partisans did their best to protect the local community. Officers from the Polish camp regularly visited the Russian camp, always bringing with them a bottle of vodka (a gesture that was rarely reciprocated), and although these meetings were outwardly cordial, there were strong undercurrents of suspicion. The Russians accused the Polish of being bad neighbours in the past, and were contemptuous of their out-dated weapons and small-scale military exploits, belittling them at every opportunity. It was true that many of the Polish weapons were out-dated – Tom had watched them dig up an old Maxim gun that took four men to lift and must already have been an antique when it was buried in 1939. Resentment was fuelled when supply loads dropped by the Allies for the Poles were stolen by the Russians, and Tom saw for himself many British boots and watches in the Soviet camp, though they never touched the British automatic weapons which they despised, particularly the Sten gun, which they considered very inferior to their own.

At night the four crewmen slept together beneath their Russian parachute, changing position every couple of nights so that they equally shared the cold outside and the warmer inside positions. They woke up one morning to a hail of machine-gun bullets thudding past their feet, fired from a Fieseler Storch which had spotted them on the ground. Most of the unit had already moved on and they were alone with Kunicki and Ducia when the attack came, sending them running for the trees. The continuous threat from the air prompted Kunicki to suggest that Tom temporarily move his crew to a gamekeepers' lodge deep in the woods, where attacks were less frequent. There was little he could do about the growing numbers of German ground troops being mobilised. Polish officers who visited the camp brought news of 24,000 second-line SS troops massing in Bilgoraj[7] to clear up the district, but added that their morale was low and they were mostly boys of fifteen to seventeen years-of-age. The good news was that Tom and Kunicki had found a field that they considered suitable for flattening into an airstrip, and this information was passed on to Kiev. Strokacz responded with a message to say that he would send an expert in airstrip construction by Dakota to check it out.[8]

On the night of the 28th May, the airmen joined Kunicki and his men at a prearranged dropping ground to await the arrival of the Russian Dakota, which was carrying airstrip specialist Lieutenant Szylowski, two female radio operators, and supplies. When the distant sound of the engine was heard Kunicki ordered the signal fires to be lit, and the prepared ground turned into a blaze of lights. A vertical 'Very' light was fired, followed by a horizontal one along the flare path, and the men rushed for cover just in case the plane was not one of theirs. The terrain-hugging Dakota came in low over the trees, and one of the partisans shouted "Ours!" as the light from the fires picked out the markings of a Soviet aircraft. One-by-one the reinforced sack containers drifted to the ground suspended beneath white silk parachutes followed by two female radio operators and Lieutenant Szylowski,

---

[7] The town of Bilgoraj was an important center of the Polish resistance, surrounded by partisan-controlled forests. The town lost 50% of its population during the War.

[8] The Russians operated the Douglas C-47 'Skytrain' (known in the UK as Dakotas) under the Lend-Lease agreement during World War II. It was the military version of the DC-3, with more powerful engines, large loading doors and utility seating along the walls. Used to carry troops and freight, it was renowned for being able to carry more than double its official payload, and was exceptionally rugged.

the airfield specialist. One of the radio operators landed so close to the fire that her parachute went up in flames, and Tom took careful note on the Russian dropping technique, which on this occasion was impressively accurate (though he felt that in general their dropping techniques were inferior to those used by his Squadron).

Partisans dispersed to recover the packages and to find Lieutenant Szylowski, who was injured in a bad landing and needed help. He was brought into the camp with his head bandaged up to a wholehearted welcome from the delighted Englishmen, who now felt sure their rescue was imminent. In the course of the next few days, delight turned to suspicion as Szylowski tried to get them drunk on vodka and spent most of the time interrogating them in the company of the political commissar, with whom he seemed particularly 'pally'. He offered to send messages back to the airmen's families, provided they used the normal RAF codes, and was keen to know the details of RAF briefings before an operation. During this questioning the crew realised that he was probably NKVD[9] and quietly tipped the vodka on the ground, or even up their sleeves; anything to remain sober. Szylowski on the other hand got very drunk and maudlin, saying to the crew: "When you come to bomb Moscow, don't bomb, land and give them my name and tell them you once lived with Russian partisans – you will be alright". The crew thought this a very odd thing for a supposed ally to say to them, but at this point Kunicki took Tom to one side and told him quietly of his own misgivings about sharing too much information with Szylowski. Kunicki and Tom had developed mutual respect during their daily treks in search of an airstrip and, although he commanded a Soviet unit, Kunicki was Polish. His loyalties must have been put to the test on many occasions.[xii] Szylowski checked out the

---

[9] Russian secret police.

chosen landing site and declared it unsuitable for a Dakota, but after a further search they found a cornfield near the village of Huta Krzeszowska that he was happy with. This posed an ethical dilemma for Kunicki, because the crop belonged to the entire village and they needed it to sustain them through the winter. It would have been a simple matter to compensate one farmer for the loss of his crop but a different prospect to pay off each individual household for their share. However this was the field selected by the expert, so Kunicki radioed the location to Kiev and decided that, if the village required compensation, he would settle the debt with cattle and grain obtained from raids. Kiev responded, and confirmed 5th June as the date for the extraction.

The proposed rescue mission gave Kunicki and his fellow Soviet commanders the opportunity to evacuate injured personnel and send important papers to Kiev and the couriers were kept busy liaising between the groups so that the best use was made of this opportunity. Meanwhile, Russian pilot Captain Vladimir Pavlov and his crew, all familiar with dangerous operations, were preparing for their most complicated assignment to date. Two Dakotas were to take part in the special operation behind enemy lines; the first to land and pick up personnel, including the British crew; the second to follow thirty minutes later and drop supplies. Pavlov, a modest and highly skilled pilot, was to carry the supplies. He carefully planned his route to take him over swampy and forested ground that he knew to be difficult for German anti-aircraft guns. In the event this proved unnecessary because they flew much of the way in thick cloud, and their main difficulty was navigating in the poor visibility. The skies cleared as they flew over the Styr River, but Navigator Dimitri Lisin could not be sure of the exact section of the river they were over to get a 'fix'. However, the crew knew that once they were spotted they would get their 'fix', because anti-aircraft guns were positioned at bridges over the river and the highway; it was just a matter of waiting. And it wasn't long before searchlights swept across the sky and tracer fire streaked past the window. Pavlov swung the plane away to the right to avoid the fire, and Lisin managed to establish his position – they were forty minutes flying time from their destination.

Preparations at the cornfield had to be left to the last minute so that the prepared ground would not be spotted by the enemy and so, on the evening of the 5th June, a partisan detachment from the area flattened and hardened the field with horse-drawn logs of wood, back and forth until the surface was solid enough to support the aircraft. Kunicki and Yakovlev's men carried out diversionary attacks on the nearby German garrisons to keep attention away from the evacuation zone, and a one-thousand strong partisan contingent surrounded the field to defend it against attack, which was sure to come once the fires were lit. Then, in the distance, the unmistakable drone of a Dakota was heard, and the prepared flare path of three bonfires was set alight to guide the aircraft in. When Pavlov arrived over the field to drop his supplies he noticed that the first aircraft, which had taken off thirty minutes ahead of him, had not arrived, and this gave him a problem. If he dropped the packages they would leave indents in the field, making it impossible for the second aircraft to land. So in a courageous manoeuvre, knowing that the injured partisans and the British crew were waiting below, he brought his aircraft down on to the prepared strip. In the darkness he was unable to find the turning circle at the end of the cleared runway, and the swirling corn chaff blocked the engine air-intakes, which began to overheat. The crew climbed out and cleared the intakes by hand as partisans arrived to direct them to the turning circle. The airmen gave their weapons to Kunicki, who would have much greater need of them, and bade him farewell. A couple of days earlier they had posed for a photograph with Kunicki and Ducia, so that proof existed that they had been alive and well when handed over,

Mikolaj 'Mucha' Kunicki.
Photo given to Tom Storey as a souvenir June 1944

and Kunicki gave Tom a photograph of himself as a souvenir. He wrote on the back, in Russian:

> "In memory of the English aviator Tom, being in my partisan unit. Brigade Commander "Stalin" (Mikolaj Kunicki) 04.06.1944, Bilgoraj forest."

Then the airmen, George, Szylowski, a group of badly-injured partisans, a pregnant woman, and important documents for Kiev were quickly loaded and Pavlov, though concerned about the excess weight of his aircraft, prepared to take off. The first two attempts failed, the Dakota stubbornly refused to move through the sandy trough into which it had settled. The engines shrieked and dust and corn chaff swirled around the plane and into the eyes of the partisans, who gathered behind the wings and tail and began to push. Heat radiated from the engines as the partisans heaved the plane until it began to move, and then Pavlov took over, slowly at first, gathering speed and, as the line of trees rushed towards them, lifting clear of the ground, almost brushing the tree tops, and disappearing into the night. The delay and the noise left the partisans on the ground exposed, and they were still trying to damp down the signal fires when two German bombers arrived over the stubble field firing heavily from machine guns and dropping bombs. Kunicki gave the order to shoot at the bombers, which eventually flew away without inflicting any casualties.

Pavlov flew close to the ground, carefully avoiding the area where they had been fired on during the outward journey, but then quite unexpectedly, a group of Germans on a riverbank below, startled by the sudden appearance of the aircraft, opened up with bursts of machine-gun fire, forcing Pavlov to throw the aircraft into a dive. The sudden manoeuvre caused injured passengers to fall from their benches and luggage to

Soviet Dakota crew: Left to Right: Vasili Kostin (2nd pilot), Dimitri Lisin (navigator), Vladimir Pavlov (captain), Ivan Shevtsov (wireless operator). Engineer Alexander Kniazkowa not shown.

tumble around them. Bullets whistled past, clunking into the metal frame, and a piece of metal flew past Tom's head and punched a hole in the cabin roof, through which a stream of air came rushing. Pavlov had his eyes glued to the ground trying to avoid the fire, while inside the blacked-out plane, one of the airmen was trying to find water for the pregnant woman, who was crying in pain. Pavlov's crew exchanged silent glances of relief when the danger had passed and Tom expressed his admiration for the skill and daring of the crew: "It was a good job", he said.

Some years later, Kunicki wrote the following words to Patrick Stradling regarding this rescue:

> "We regarded you as the luckiest people in the world that I succeeded to get you out, because I do not know what would happen to you, whether your families and England would ever see you, because the bullets do not choose. It is a matter of fact I often said in those hard times, when we were encircled, that it was a good thing that I sent you away, but it would be better for me to have Paddy at my side because he was a very good shooter of all kinds of firearms. In those battles not only were four additional partisans of great help, but also even one man was of great significance."[xiii]

Eddie and Hap had been transported by cattle truck to Stalag Luft 6, in East Prussia (now Lithuania), where they received their POW numbers – 3694 for Eddie, and 3607 for Hap. Not a comfortable journey on a passenger train this time, but a cramped and uncomfortable four-day trip in a cattle truck. In fact they were treated like cattle, even down to the straw on the floor of the truck. The camp held a few thousand British, American, Canadian, and Polish Air Force prisoners-of-war, and the senior British NCO running things was Warrant Officer James 'Dixie' Deans, a bomber pilot who spoke fluent

German and commanded the respect of both the prisoners and their guards at the Heyderkrug camp. Red Cross parcels were received regularly, with a proportion of the contents going to the cookhouse to ensure that everyone had at least one meal a day, and other items kept back for bartering with some of the guards. They were interrogated by special investigators on the 17th May, along with another RAF crew, who they then didn't see again. Thinking they may have been moved on for more intensive questioning, Eddie and Hap were concerned for their welfare and raised the matter with Deans, who reassured them: "Don't worry, Red Cross keep a special eye on you chaps".[xiv]

There was no Red Cross to keep an eye on Walter, who was living a precarious existence, constantly in fear of being discovered by German patrols that would suddenly arrive at the house, or swoop on the village and take young people for slave labour. Daily life at the cottage was hard, but despite the Germans having taken most of their cows, they had two left and Mrs Dec made butter from the milk and they had eggs from the hens. Walter learned to forage for mushrooms, some of which could provide an entire meal for the family. Even poisonous fungi were gathered to use as a fly-killer on the windowsill. Forest fruits and leaves were collected for making tea, and Mr Dec grew tobacco plants, drying the leaves on top of the bread oven. Walter found it hard to watch his '*matka*' struggle through her daily chores, and on one occasion tried to help as she walked barefoot to the fields carrying a load on her back and pushing a sack truck with her feet. Mr Dec immediately intervened and gave the load back to his wife, and Walter had to learn not to interfere in a way of life which had rules beyond his comprehension. In June he was visited by a Home Army officer from Warsaw, who gave him 5,000 zloty, and told him to 'lie low' and to expect an aircraft. His hopes of rescue were raised, but no aircraft arrived. His days in the Dec family home were drawing to a close, and it was with a sense of apprehension that he listened to the sound of the approaching Russian army. He still naively believed that, being Allies, everything would be alright once they arrived, but the next phase of his ordeal was just beginning.[xv] Back home in England, his parents and fiancée Winnie received clandestine information that Walter was safe and living on a farm in Poland, though this information was to be kept secret for fear of comprising his safety and that of his protectors. There would be a long wait for his homecoming.[xvi]

CHAPTER 8

THE JOURNEY HOME

It was still dark as the Dakota flew low over the ruined streets of Kiev, with its silent anti-aircraft guns still pointing skyward. The Soviet army had retaken the city five months earlier, but the retreating Germans had set about its methodical destruction as they left. Pavlov brought his Dakota down on to the desolate runway, and almost immediately, an ambulance arrived to collect the injured passengers and the pregnant woman to take them to hospital. As he left the plane, Tom picked up the jagged piece of metal that had almost killed him and put it in his pocket as a souvenir. Three black limousines rolled up next, and the crew were greeted on the tarmac by General Strokacz and his entourage of uniformed officers (and an interpreter). After a short speech, Strokacz shook their hands and gave them the news that Allied forces had just landed on the beaches of Normandy – Operation Overlord had begun. The mood was celebratory as Tom thanked Pavlov and his crew, and said goodbye to George, who had been extremely nervous throughout the flight having joined it without clearance from the Soviet authorities. He had come to plead for Russian supplies and backup for his Polish unit, and hoped that the company of the British airmen would afford him official status.

The four men were driven to the run-down Intourist Hotel in Kiev where they enjoyed a hot bath with scrubbing brushes, followed by breakfast of caviar, omelette, and vodka. They remained under close surveillance in the hotel for a week, only being allowed out once a day for fresh air, but they were treated well and given fresh clothes. They were finally able to climb out of the RAF battledress they had worn for the last seven weeks. A cinema screen was set up in the hotel and they watched 'The Jungle Book' in English; a simple pleasure that delighted them after weeks of struggling to understand conversations around them. Strokacz asked Tom what they had been doing in Poland, but didn't press the subject when no response was forthcoming, and he went on to deflect questions from a local press correspondent, saying that it was no use asking questions because the men would not be able to answer. After a week in Kiev Tom and his crew were flown, by Pavlov, into Moscow, where Lieutenant General Montagu Burrows, head of the British Military Mission, had just been informed by his Soviet liaison counterpart, General Slavin,[1] that they were on their way.

Kunicki meanwhile had settled his account with the villagers of Huta Krzeszowska for the destruction of their corn crop and, since they had gallantly refused compensation, he gave instead medicines and access to his unit doctors along with the use of redundant materials, such as old harnesses and parachutes.[i] The villagers may have felt that the sacrifice of their corn was a small price to pay for the protection of a well-equipped fighting unit such as that of Kunicki and his fellow Soviet commanders as Operation STURMWIND got underway. Fighting broke out within days of the airmen's departure, and the odds against the 3,000-strong combined Polish and Soviet units were overwhelming. A German force of around 40,000 was closing in with a single objective: to clear the partisans from the forest. In spite of these odds, the Polish and Soviet units cooperated under the command of Soviet General Prokupiak, and fought a courageous campaign culminating, on the 14th June, in a battle at Porytowe Hill.

[1] Head of Directorate for Soviet liaison with Allies, General Staff.

Here the partisans formed a defensive circle two kilometres in diameter and blocked all approach roads with mines and felled trees. When the onslaught began, it was with such terrifying force that, throughout the day and late into the night, there was hardly a second without gunfire. Trees ripped out of the ground by their roots sprang high into the air as the Germans attacked with tanks, aircraft, artillery and infantry.[ii] Smoke flares added to the choking smog on that hot June day, and the Kalmucks, a fearsome band of Mongol horsemen fighting with the Germans, struck fear into the staunchest partisan hearts as they rode across the cornfields on their small, black horses, screaming in a strange tongue.[iii] The partisans eventually ran out of water and, with hands and faces burning from the heat of their gun barrels, they were forced to cool them with their own urine. After the artillery and mortar barrage, the Germans made two breaks in the defensive circle, but the attacks were driven back, and overnight the partisans managed to break out of the encirclement and move forty kilometres east, to the village of Osuchy. STURMWIND I had failed. The partisans had broken out of the encirclement and regrouped ready to continue the fight, though losses were high and included that of Kunicki's wireless operator, Ducia.

In Moscow, the imminent arrival of four British airmen caused a flurry of activity at the British Military Mission HQ, and General Burrows asked his Air Attaché, Commodore David Roberts, to contact the Air Ministry in Whitehall as a matter of urgency, to verify the identities of the four men. He urged Roberts to stress the importance of an immediate reply, adding: "I shall be interested to hear these fellows' stories, and I think we can 'make much' of this case by insisting on getting them back as soon as possible." Roberts duly sent the following message to the Air Ministry in Whitehall:

"Urgently request immediate confirmation if these names tally with those of any missing crews. Consider extremely important bona fides be verified earliest possible as Russians most – repeat – most suspicious any ruse on part of enemy to plant agents."[iv]

Relieved to be a step nearer home and unaware of the stir they were causing, Tom and the crew were driven to a dingy office in a back street and given a meal, before being taken to the British Mission HQ, where they were led down a long corridor and through double doors into a room with a huge table. There sat a number of people, including General Burrows and Commodore Roberts. They were formally handed over, with a letter from General Slavin, which read:

> "I have the honour to hand over [these men] in accordance with instructions issued by the Supreme Command of the RED Army, to the BRITISH Military Mission to the USSR for disposal."

The men were questioned for about an hour, with an interpreter translating their words for the benefit of the high-ranking Russian officers present. Two days later Tom went through a lengthy debrief with Brigadier George Hill, Head of the SOE Mission in Moscow, which focused mainly on the composition, equipment, and morale of the partisan groups he had spent time with and, in particular, relations between Polish and Soviet units. During the discussion, Tom mentioned that his crew's identities had been checked and accepted by the Russians at the time they were handed over to Kunicki's unit (the 'Curly Brown' signals), which surprised Hill because the first the British Mission had known of them was the message from Slavin the day before they landed in Moscow. That afternoon, Brigadier Hill passed this information on to General Burrows, who was outraged at the lack of cooperation from the Russians, and asked Roberts to check it with the Air Ministry, adding: "If it is true, they [the Russians] gave us unnecessary labour, and I can no longer feel that they trusted us 100% as I had hoped"[v]. Roberts accordingly sent an enquiry to Whitehall:

> "Please confirm Russians did not first get their Mission in London to verify bona fides with you as it seems from statement of aircrew, Russians were well satisfied their true identity before they reached Moscow."[vi]

The response to this message is not available, but clearly the Mission staff in Moscow were angry at having been misled over the issue of the airmen's identities. General Burrows had only been in his post for three months, and was already finding that any contact with the Soviet general staff, however urgent, had to go through a liaison section that would not fix meetings in advance, acknowledge correspondence, or even inform the British Mission when they were out of Moscow. Relations were very strained. Burrows had initially thought that his weakened position was a consequence of the delayed Allied invasion of France, and hoped that his standing would improve once OVERLORD got underway, but it quickly became apparent that it made no difference, and relations continued in: "an atmosphere of unbounded suspicion"[vii]. This disquiet did not prevent him from writing, with diplomatic correctness, a gracious letter of thanks to General Slavin for promptly delivering the four aviators to the British Mission. He expressed his admiration for the Soviet partisan units, and in particular that of Mikolaj Kunicki, to whom he enclosed a letter of thanks.[viii]

By this time, the 24th June, the partisans were encircled for a second time in the village of Osuchy (STURMWIND II), and whereas Kunicki's men managed to break out after bitter fighting, the Polish units, including those of Father John and Kmicic, did not. Cooperation between the Soviet and Polish commands had broken down during this tragic battle, and the Polish units found themselves trapped deep in the forest when

German ground troops entered the woods. The result was a devastating defeat, and Nina later wrote that towards the end of the action, when nothing else was left, "Partisans were fighting with knives, fists and teeth"[ix]. Two brave participants in the STURMWIND campaign were Nina and her mother, who returned to their family home, on the Solski hunting estate, when it became the German Command Centre, in order to gather intelligence. Ingratiating themselves with the officers by cleaning, running errands, and gathering fresh fruit in the forest for their table, they gathered reports on troop movements, including maps and detailed tactical plans, and smuggled food and dressings to the wounded men and women who were hidden in caves, behind waterfalls, and in quarries. Nina recalled that some of the wounded were hidden, by their comrades, in trees – strapped to the branches. Sometimes those friends were killed in battle, leaving no one to bring them down before they died, and eventually their bones fell from the trees.[x] Kunicki, having broken out of the encirclement, was surrounded for a third time near Lvov, where his unit spent eight days without water or bread, eating raw horsemeat to survive. Again he broke out and, after many battles and marches, his detachment reached the Carpathian Mountains, and went on to fight in Hungary and Czechoslovakia.

In July, General Burrows' letter of thanks to Kunicki reached him:

> "As Chief of the British Military Mission in Moscow, I am writing to you to tell you that the Soviet general staff handed over to me the four British aviators who spent several weeks with you in your territory. They arrived safe and sound, and their well-being reflects the greatest credit on the care you and your partisans took of them. They are full of admiration of the skill with which you are damaging our common enemy, the Germans, and for your admirable organisation, which

enabled you to pass them back through the German lines. On behalf of the British Navy, Army and Air Force, I would like to send to you, partisan leader Mikolaj Kunicki, and your brave partisans, my best thanks and my best wishes for your success and speedy reunion with the Red Army.[xi]

Meanwhile efforts turned to repatriating the aircrew. The Air Ministry had requested that the crew should be returned to the UK at the earliest opportunity, and Admiral Archer[2] asked the senior British naval officer to North Russia to arrange passage to UK for the four men. Tom and the crew were issued with new passports stamped with Russian visas, and on 26th June embarked on the three-day train journey to Murmansk to join HMS Matchless, which together with destroyers HMS Meteor and Musketeer, was preparing to leave Scapa Flow on Operation DOG CHARLIE: the delivery of mail and supplies to Kola Inlet. HMS Matchless was a destroyer of the Home Fleet that plied the Arctic convoy route between Scapa Flow and the Kola Inlet in the far north of Russia. She had, just a few months earlier, been involved in the sinking of the German battleship Scharnhorst, which had been about to leave her Norwegian base to attack the convoys. The crew of HMS Matchless had pulled six German sailors out of the icy water on that occasion, and they were about to take four more servicemen to safety.[xii] Matchless arrived in Murmansk on the 3rd July, and left the following day for Scapa Flow carrying the four RAF passengers and escorted for the first 70 miles by Russian fighter aircraft. Back at the British Mission in Moscow, Commodore Roberts, who had spoken with Tom at length of his experiences with the partisans, felt that Kunicki's role in the rescue merited some acknowledgement, and he wrote to the British Ambassador to Moscow,

_____
[2] Naval Attaché at the Moscow Mission.

Sir Archibald Clark-Kerr, to ask him about the possibility of recognising his courage and initiative with some kind of award, adding: "I personally would like to see you pin a Military Cross on him". Sir Archibald agreed that Kunicki deserved recognition, and offered to write privately to Anthony Eden at the Foreign Office to see if something could be done for him. I don't believe Kunicki received anything more than a letter of thanks, but it was undoubtedly his decisive action that got the airmen out of the forest before STURMWIND got underway, after which their chances of survival would have been slim.

On the 8th July, 1944, the aircrew disembarked at Scapa Flow and were classed as 'fit repatriated RAF personnel from enemy occupied territory', given a £5 advance of pay, and told to proceed immediately, without breaking their journey under any circumstance, to the London District Transit Camp No.1.[xiii] This was not as grim as it sounds, as the camp was The Great Central Hotel in Marylebone, but the order not to break their journey was a cruel one for Tom, who would have to pass through his home town of Carlisle without being able to visit his family. His parents, Mary and Joe, had no intention of missing their son however, and went to the railway station at Carlisle to wait on the platform, where they managed to snatch a few minutes with him as the train pulled in to take on passengers. On arrival at Transit Camp No.1, and just three days after disembarking HMS Matchless in Scapa Flow, Tom began two days of debriefing by various branches of the intelligence services[3], a Russian liaison group, and MO1 (SP), the cover name for SOE.[xiv]

Finally he was granted home leave, and he returned to the Unicorn Hotel Ludlow for a reunion with Rita. It was just ten

---

[3] MI5, MI3, IS9(W) and IS9(X).

months since he had flown off to join his Squadron in North Africa, and yet it was a lifetime. Although back in body, his mind churned with thoughts of his lost crew members and the partisans who he had left in such a perilous situation. To the parents of Walter Davis he wrote:

> "I was the pilot and captain of the aircraft from which your son Walter was reported missing. I am unable to give you any information regarding him except that he left the aircraft and reached the ground safely. If you have received any information about him, would you please let me know? I was fortunate enough to escape. Unfortunately we were widely separated and I was unable to get in touch with Walter. Immediately upon my escape I asked permission to be dropped in his vicinity to assist him, but this was refused."

He travelled north to the family home in Carlisle, 5 Belah Road, Stanwix, where his entire family had gathered to welcome him home, posing for a photograph in the garden. After this brief reunion he was ordered back to London for a meeting with Poland's Prime Minister in exile, Stanislaw Mikolajczk, at the Polish Embassy in London. His days were filled with administrative tasks and letter writing, but every night in dreams he struggled to keep his aircraft in flight, fought off enemies, and waded through swamps to find his crew. He thrashed about in the grip of nightmares, and in the morning peace of mind was fleeting. He wanted to go back into Poland and find Walter Davis, the first member of his crew and great friend, but instead he was told to report to Morecambe on the 2nd September for re-kitting, and to await posting. The seaside town of Morecambe, with its narrow streets of boarding houses, theatres, and famous sunset over the bay, would one day be significant to Tom, but in October 1944, it was just a holding camp, and a step in his progression back to operational flying. When his posting came through however, it was not to

The Storey family at 5 Belah Road, Stanwix, Carlisle

an operational squadron, but to 32 Maintenance Unit, RAF St. Athan where, because of his flying experience, he was given the job of Unit Test Pilot.

Walter, still in Poland, had listened to the sounds of the Russian Army getting closer during the early summer of 1944, and thought his troubles would soon be at an end. In fact they got much worse and, as the front came closer, he found himself in no-man's land, and took to sheltering in an underground potato store as the shells flew overhead. He watched German Stukas dive-bombing a nearby village, and then at the end of July began to see the first Russian soldiers. An officer took over his room in the Dec's house, and although he was given a document by the AK Home Army, certifying his nationality, the Russians didn't recognise the AK as a legal organisation, making his papers worthless. One by one, AK officers in the area were rounded up and shot, including the farmer who had carried him to Smolarzyna in a cart. The structure that had saved and nurtured him was crumbling into pieces, and Walter, who had hoped for help from the Russians, found himself hiding from them in fear for his life. In September, Polish militia, who had collaborated with the Russians, came to arrest the Dec's son, and also asked for Walter Davis. At this point, Private Jimmy Bloom arrived back on the scene with two bicycles, declaring that it was too dangerous to stay in the village, and the two men cycled to the town of Lancut, where, once again, they were taken in and sheltered for several weeks by two Polish families in the town. Every knock on the door meant scuttling to a hiding place, but this time they were hiding from the Russians.

In the New Year of 1945, Walter and Jimmy moved to a room in the house of Mr Szust, in Lancut, and Walter was able to attend church from time-to-time and on one occasion, even to play the church organ. He remembered being very moved by a requiem mass for the victims of the Warsaw massacre, at which the entire congregation wept loudly. They moved to the larger town of Rzeszow when they heard that American servicemen were awaiting evacuation from there, but they arrived too late for the aircraft, which had just taken off. Rzeszow was full of prisoners of war who had recently been freed from German camps by the Russians, and it was here that they met up with two members of Walter's Squadron, Alan Jolly and Robert Peterson, survivors of the McCall crew, who had been shot down in August flying supplies to the Home Army near Krakow. Three of their crew had been killed and the other four had baled out and were on the run. Davis, Jolly and Peterson stayed together from this point on, and in order to avoid divulging the nature of their missions, they made up the story that they had been bombing in Upper Silesia, and stuck to it whenever questioned. Bloom was in the greatest danger because of his time fighting with the AK, and the Russians were actively looking for him under his Polish identity, Antoni Sawicki. He was taken in for questioning, and only released when Walter and a group of ex POWs spoke up for him and said he was one of them. At this point, Bloom, who had no wish to fall into Russian hands again, took off, returning to the Polish partisans in Lancut, with the parting words to his friends: "We will all end up in Siberia".[xv]

The Russians knew the names of Allied servicemen they were likely to find because staff at the British Mission in Moscow had compiled a list of army and RAF personnel known to be in Poland, either as evaders or prisoners of war, and a copy of this was given to General Slavin so that his troops could identify and give news of them to the British Mission. On that list were the names of missing members of the McCall and Storey crews, and Private Bloom of the East Kent Regiment,[xvi] but with no Allied organisation to assist them, they were issued with Russian uniforms and moved on in a dislocated muddle, by cattle truck or on foot, with little food and no means of cooking any they had. Their progress took them firstly to Jaslo, then on to Nowy Sacz and Przemysl, from where Walter remembered walking across the frozen River San to Lvov. From Lvov, they caught a train to Kiev and then to Odessa, where finally they embarked on the old cruise liner, the Duchess of Bedford. Walter had seen terrible suffering on his journey; he had been cold and desperately hungry, but finally he was back in British hands, and exchanged his Russian uniform for RAF khaki. It was the 14th March 1945, and he and his companions, Alan Jolly and Robert Peterson, were on their way home.

By this time, the Russians had given British Mission personnel permission to visit Lublin to try and locate Allied evaders and POWs, but this came too late to help Walter and his fellow travellers, who had already made the journey to Odessa in abject conditions. As it transpired the British Mission was also unable to assist remaining Allied personnel because of resolute stonewalling by the Russians. Burrows felt that permission to visit Lublin was only granted to give the impression that they were honouring agreements. They were effectively denied access to the ex-POWs who were being held at collecting points by the Russians. Relations had not improved, and Burrows wrote cynically of this episode:

> "Meantime it looks as if the Russians have been despatching to Odessa all the ex-POWs they can find, hoping to get Poland cleared before their non-observance of the agreement leads to a showdown in Moscow."[xvii]

The men sailed to Malta in the Duchess of Bedford, and then transferred to the troop ship RMS Orion in Valetta Harbour. This took them to Gibraltar, where they joined a convoy escorted by destroyers for the final leg of the voyage through dangerous U-boat patrolled waters. When the commodore aboard the Orion heard that three airmen on board had been with the Polish underground, he sent for them and, after listening to their story, broke the strict 'no alcohol' regulation, and gave them a beer.

Eddie Elkington-Smith arrived back on home soil two months later in a Lancaster Bomber of 106 Squadron, having become separated from Hap during their long march to freedom. With the approach of the Russians in July 1944, Stalag Luft VI was evacuated, and Eddie and Hap were taken on foot and by cattle train to Thorn, in Poland, and then on to Stammlager 357 at Fallingbostel, in West Germany. At this camp, seventeen thousand prisoners of war, most of them British, were crammed into huts designed to hold a third of that number, and food shortages were acute. The Germans, despite being in retreat, were determined to prevent the liberation of their prisoners, and nine months later this camp too was evacuated, and 12,000 British POWs, including the camp leader 'Dixie Deans', were marched away to the north east in columns of 2,000. Eddie and Hap became separated during the long trek, with Hap's group arriving at the village of Gresse, east of the Elbe, after ten days of forced marching. Here, Hap witnessed the death of a young RAF sergeant, Kenneth Mortimer, who was shot and killed, along with about thirty other prisoners, when their lines were mistaken for a German troop column and strafed by British Typhoons. There was no camp at the end of this march, and they were finally liberated by British troops near Lubeck on the 2nd May, 1945. Eddie made his own way to an aerodrome in Rheine, from where he was flown home.[xviii]

Within days of the return of Eddie and Hap, Tom and Rita's first child, daughter Patricia, was born, and the following month he was awarded a 'Mention in Despatches' for his actions following the loss of his aircraft. The lost crew were all back on home soil, but the Squadron had suffered terrible losses attempting to take supplies into Warsaw during the August uprising, and many of his friends were dead. Tom's thoughts constantly returned to the Squadron and to his partisan companions in Poland, with whom he had no contact since leaving them prior to STURMWIND. He tried to find some of them with the help of the Polish Red Cross, but this proved difficult as the partisans operated under codenames, but they did manage to put him in touch with his friend and interpreter Alojzego Pajaka (Ali), who had survived the battle, but was captured by the Germans and had spent time in a concentration camp. Tom wrote to Ali and tried to explain that although his Squadron had done their best, and many of his friends had been killed delivering supplies to Warsaw, the obstacles were just too great. "Whatever you think of politicians, positive or negative, remember one thing Ali, those English boys gave their lives to help their friends."[xix] He spoke fondly of the songs that George and the partisans had taught him, saying that he had not forgotten one of them, and he asked Ali to tell all his comrades that he would love to hear from them and receive photographs.

It would be twelve years before news of George would reach his friends in England, but in May 1945 as the last members of the

Storey crew were making their way home, he was fighting with the Polish Second Army as it progressed from Berlin to Dresden, and then Prague. After separating from the crew at Kiev Aerodrome, George had succeeded in getting General Strokacz' approval to return to the Polish forests with a team of people equipped by the Soviets, to work under Kunicki's command, but in a cruel twist of fate, STURMWIND fighting broke out before he was able to return. He waited daily for news of the battle, but it soon became clear that Kunicki was not in a position to receive air drops, and Strokacz cancelled the planned mission. George was instead drafted into the Russian airborne division, and two weeks later parachuted into the Carpathian Mountains from a Dakota flown by the Pavlov crew. He was wounded in battle but his injuries were light, and he was passed over the front to the Polish Second Army. Wounded again, this time seriously, George's war was also over, but his trials were not.

CHAPTER 9

HOME

Peace returned to Europe in May 1945, just two days after my sister Pat was born, and it was a time of change for war-weary people. Churchill's Conservative Government was very quickly swept out of power in a landslide election victory for Labour, whose pledge of full employment for returning servicemen and a 'cradle-to-grave' health service struck a chord after the hardship of war. Thousands of servicemen would never return; their fate and whereabouts unknown, but Walter Davis, the last missing member of the Storey crew, made it home to his parents' house in time for VE day and, by way of celebration, hung a notice outside next to the Union Jack that read *Niech żyje Polska* (Long Live Poland). His friend, Private Jimmy Bloom eventually reported to the British Embassy in Warsaw and worked there as in interpreter for five weeks before being repatriated in October 1945. In 1947 he received the British Empire Medal for gallant and distinguished services in the field.[i] Tom continued to fly with the RAF for another year, before a failed eye test grounded him and he was moved to a desk job. His old crew would attest to the fact that his eyesight had always been pretty bad, joking that his landings were better at night than in the day, but in peacetime, it was no longer expedient to overlook such imperfection. Life in the RAF without flying was unthinkable, so Tom resigned his commission, returning to Ludlow where he took over the running of the Unicorn Hotel with Rita. There followed a series of unsettled and restless years, with job opportunities ill-matched to his skills or potential. He yearned for a better life and, having done his pilot training in Canada and mixed with many Canadians who flew with the Squadron, decided that he and Rita should emigrate. Charlie Keen had already left for Canada and was flying with the Transatlantic Ferry Unit, and Patrick Stradling would also take his family to Canada and then to Rhodesia in the 1950s. Tom's plan was well advanced when Rita became ill, spending many weeks in hospital and, having given up the tenancy of The Unicorn, he was forced to look for whatever job he could get, and that job was an assistant in an ironmonger's shop.

His next job was as a food inspector, which suited him better because he could keep on the move, but his mind always returned to Poland, and the friends he had left behind. Any news of Poland in the national newspapers caught his eye, and he read that Stanislaw Mikolajczyk, who had returned to Poland in 1945 as a Deputy Prime Minister, had fled back to England, having been unable to protect his country from Communist domination. He had met Mikolajczyk in 1944, and his plight prompted Tom to write him a letter, sympathising with his situation and saying: "I am happy that you have sought refuge in this country, as I did with your people". Mikolajczyk very quickly moved on to America, where he settled, but he remembered Tom, and took the time to reply and wish him well before leaving. And then, in April 1947, just a few months before I was born, the body of Peter Crosland was found on a wooded hillside in the Cabar district of Yugoslavia, where it had lain since November, 1943. The woodsmen who found him buried his remains on the hillside, retaining the identity tags, which enabled one of the RAF search parties (MRES[1]) to locate his body during a sweep of Yugoslavia, and re-inter his body in the Belgrade War

---

[1] Missing Research and Enquiry Service.

Cemetery. Tom read about it in a national newspaper and wrote to the RAF to confirm that the story was true, later travelling to London to identify some of Peter's personal effects.

The family continued to grow with the birth of my younger sister Susan in 1949, and by this time we were living in an 'Airey House'[2] on the outskirts of Ludlow, which was a good place for a young family, and we loved it. The football pitch was at the bottom of our road, Clee View, and every Saturday we walked down to watch from the touchline as Dad, always taller than anyone around him, streaked down the pitch flicking the ball between his feet, and weaving through the opposition. At around this time we acquired an old Austin car, in which we would travel to Carlisle to visit our Cumbrian family. Wrapped in blankets, we would be loaded into the car at bedtime so that we could sleep, but somehow we always managed to be awake for the thrill of Shap Fell. It was a long haul to the top of this barren section of the A6, and in the dark it seemed to us bleakest and most frightening place we could imagine. My memory always had us driving through fog, sleet, or lashing rain. The lights of oncoming cars would be blinding, and yet Dad never flinched or appeared worried; these were the conditions that were familiar for him and he seemed completely at ease. I remember once on a particularly bad night asking him how he could see where he was going. He said: "I keep my eyes lowered on the left edge of the road, and I never look at the lights". We loved his reassuring presence because he made the frightening feel normal, and we would arrive in Carlisle, having overcome the perils of Shap, feeling like adventurers ourselves.

It was the move to Lancaster in the north west of England that really changed everything, and yet it was a very positive move

---

[2] Post war prefabricated house.

to a beautiful part of the country. Dad had got a job as a travelling salesman for Jewsbury and Brown, soft drinks merchant, and not only did the job come with a house and a car, but the move, close to the sea at Morecambe, was hopefully going to help Susan, who suffered from chronic asthma and had spent long months in a sanatorium before the move. This was an ideal job for Dad, who loved being behind the wheel of a car, and had an easy-going, genial manner that enabled him to develop a rapport with the managers of the busy theatres and piers in the seaside town of Morecambe, which formed his 'patch'. For him, it was a bit like being back in the RAF mess, propping up the bar at the Winter Gardens, the Alhambra, the Gaumont, and the Central Pier, and for us there was the thrill of him arriving home with our autograph books signed by the stars of the day; Jerry Colunna, Alma Cogan, and most thrilling of all, Tommy Steele. On one occasion, when Susan was confined to bed with a severe asthma attack, Dad brought Harold Graham, the organist from the Central Pier and well-known local celebrity to visit and cheer her up, and on another occasion he got us complimentary tickets for 'Dancing Waters' at the Gaumont. Coloured jets of water, dancing to the 1812 overture, would be a laughable entertainment now, but we were thrilled by the spectacle, especially when the manager treated us to a box of chocolates in the interval. The fifties were great years for the seaside towns, and although they began well for us, it wasn't long before clouds began to gather. Coming home from school, more often than not, Dad would be sitting by the fire and not at work. I say he was there, but actually he had begun to retreat to his 'other place', and we became quite used to it. The anniversary of the ill-fated flight in April was always a difficult time for him and seemed to intensify his emotional turmoil. Then, in September 1957, he was unsettled by an advertisement that had been placed in The Times:

"Greetings to pilot and crew of RAF bomber who, on a mission from Brindisi over Poland 1942, were forced down River San. Stayed with partisans at Ulanow until taken over to Allies by Russians in July 1944. From partisan commander."

Who had placed this strange advert, and why? About this time, their old partisan friend George got in touch and, in an exchange of correspondence with Patrick Stradling, warned that they should not respond to The Times notice, saying: "The Soviet partisan who sent you to Russia [Kunicki] is now living in Poland, not wanting to stay in Russia. He was in prison too. He was not the author of the greetings!" George explained that he had been unable to get in touch any sooner because he had been seriously wounded while fighting with the Polish Second Army in Czechoslovakia towards the end of the war, and had spent months in a military hospital. He had returned to the army after discharge from hospital, reaching the rank of Major and then, in 1951, he was arrested on political charges. There followed three years of investigation, after which he was given a prison sentence of twelve years.[3ii] At the time of making contact with the British men, he was working with a foreign trade organisation, and had begun to write an account of his years with the partisans.[4] He asked for details of the crash and information about the crew to assist with this memoir, but Tom took the cautious approach, and did not respond to the letter. It had arrived with a covering note from the Air Attaché in Warsaw, saying: "You would be best advised at this stage to write in terms of happiness at having contact again and not reveal any names of other crew or information which might not be permitted to be passed by Air Ministry."

Tom was unsettled during this period, feeling threatened and nervous if a stranger came to the door, telling Rita: "Don't answer, just in case". However irrational his fear seemed,

---

[3] He was released after four years.
[4] 'Wierchami Karpat', which was published in 1964.

he really thought that the Russians were trying to find him. Group Captain Ridgway, Air Attaché in Warsaw, wrote to all four men with regard to The Times item, advising them not to reveal any information about their aircraft, the crash, or their experiences, until he contacted them again, and suggested that if they needed to get in touch with him, they should only do so via the Foreign Office because: "Letters through the open post will definitely be censored". These were the Cold War years, and the "atmosphere of unbounded suspicion" that Burrows had spoken of was no longer confined to Moscow. Rita kept the house- hold running during Tom's crisis, but then one day the company car disappeared and a stack of cardboard boxes appeared for us to pack our belongings in. "Where are we going, Mum?" She smiled, and said: "I'm not sure yet". Now she was the calm, reassuring voice that made everything seem alright.

Tom Storey with his daughters 1957

We moved to a boarding house in Morecambe and, although we had not planned to take in visitors, when a family of holidaymakers knocked on the door and asked if we had any rooms, Mum thought: "Well, why not?" We were clearly not business people because we ended up accommodating one or two long-term boarders who had fallen on hard times, and were unable to pay for their lodging. One was a musician from the Joe Loss Orchestra, who was sacked while playing with the band on the Central Pier. His one-week stay turned into weeks as he worked on his legal case for wrongful dismissal, promising to pay for his lodging when he won the case. Pat spent many hours writing and rewriting pages of evidence for him, but it came to nothing and he eventually moved on. Dad managed to get his job back briefly, and it seemed that things were looking up, but it didn't last, and he seemed quite broken by the weight of responsibility and his inability to get well. Mum got an extra job as manageress of a new café attached to Twell's corner shop, and because of that, when we suddenly had to move from the boarding house following the death of the landlord, we were offered the flat above the shop and café. I could see the forecourt of the Central Pier from my bedroom window, and we were all quietly pleased to have escaped the boarding house business, which none of us had enjoyed. Free time was spent leading donkey rides along the sands and searching for the pennies that used to fall from the slot machines on the pier, dropping through the planking and onto the wet sand beneath. I joined the Sea Cadets during this period, and loved to march along the promenade playing a bugle in the band, but we also took summer jobs, which was an easy thing to do in a seaside town. One blissful summer of 1959, Pat and I were sent to Ireland to stay with Mum's sister and our Irish cousins in Killybegs, Donegal. What a joyful, free-spirited summer that was.

Then life over the shop came to a sudden end when Mr Twell, the owner, closed up one night, put the contents of the till in his pocket, and walked out. He simply disappeared, and it was many years before we learned that he had caught the Heysham ferry to Belfast and begun a new life in Ireland. At the time we had no idea what had happened to him. The shop and café closed and we were on the move again. This final move was to a house at Hest Bank, a 'passing through' sort of place on the A6 between Morecambe and Carnforth. We managed to get the house at an affordable rent because the owners had suffered a terrible tragedy when their only child was killed on the busy A6, which ran along the bottom of the road. They moved out as soon as we agreed to move in and, although the house seemed to harbour grief, Dad seemed happier as he dug and tended a vegetable plot in the private back garden, which shielded him from the outside world and, most of all, from anyone who called at the house. He spent hours digging, raking, planting, and weeding, and the absorption seemed to lift his spirits. He got us an old canvas canoe to mess about in on the canal and talked a local farmer into giving us a Border collie, which in the absence of any sheep, took to rounding up the two pet rabbits that ran free in the garden and played havoc with the vegetable plot.

We caught the school bus into Lancaster every day and life was a whirlwind of friends, homework, and the nightly ritual of jiggling the TV aerial so that we could get a good enough picture to watch Top of the Pops, or Ready Steady Go. Every Sunday, Mum would cook a roast, which Dad would carve. He always had fresh vegetables from his garden plot, and from time to time they sang together as the food was prepared. There were flashes of life as it used to be, when Dad would play the mouth-organ for us as a treat at bedtime, "D'ye ken John Peel with his coat so gay…", or dance around the room singing a silly song. We clung on to these happy moments because they were increasingly rare, and what we knew, but couldn't express, was that Dad was by now only partly with us. It was the fire now that absorbed him almost totally. He would sit hunched over it and stare into the flames for hours, sometimes until it died and went cold, and still we would chatter and sing and argue as though nothing was wrong. He had aged far beyond his years, and his physical health was also beginning to fail, with a collapsed lung and long bouts of illness. Once a week he would put on a suit and catch the bus into Lancaster to queue at the Labour Exchange in the hope of finding work, but he would not work again.

When the end came, it was unexpected. Even with such intimate knowledge of his mental and physical health, we were not prepared. Pat had just started work as a lab assistant at the technical college, which is where she was on the Thursday that it happened. Dad's brother, John Storey, had called in the early afternoon and he had done his best to find words of encouragement and motivation as he sat at the bedside. Mum took a cup of tea up shortly after the visit and placed it gently on the floor by the bed – Tom appeared to be asleep. She was in the kitchen as Susan and I arrived home on the school bus. It must have been around half past four, and we dropped our bags on the floor and went running upstairs to see Dad, where we found him dead. Pat got a call at work to tell her to go home straight away, and as she walked through the front door, Dad's body was being brought down the stairs. From that moment on we were bonded to each other by the tragedy and the profound sense of loss, which was almost never talked about from that day on. We didn't talk about it outside the house, and we didn't talk about it amongst ourselves. We wrapped a protective cloak of silence around it; a silence that lasted for years.

A crew reunion took place the year after Dad's death as a result of a personal notice in the Daily Mirror. The item was placed by Ivan Shevtsov, radio operator on the Pavlov crew, who wanted to meet up with the airmen he had flown to safety in June 1944. The newspaper managed to trace Jim Hughes, Charlie Keen and Patrick Stradling, who were reunited with Shevtsov in March 1965 in London, in the company of Pravda correspondent, Oleg Orestov, and a Daily Mirror reporter. The subsequent article titled: 'The Great Reunion of the Englishman, the Irishman, the Welshman and the Ukrainian' made a full-page spread, and mentioned that the pilot, Thomas Storey, had not been traced for the reunion. None of them knew that Tom was dead and, maybe more remarkably, they believed that Walter had been shot by the Germans and had no idea that he had eventually made it home and was alive. Walter read the story of the reunion in the Daily Mirror and immediately made contact with his fellow crew members. Rita also read the article, with some sadness since Tom could never be part of his crew again, and she contacted the Daily Mirror to tell them of his death. Charlie Keen and Jim Hughes very quickly made their way to the home of Walter Davis in Kent for a second reunion, and the news of Tom's death was given to them by the Daily Mirror reporter. It was the 23rd April, 1965, twenty-one years to the day after baling out. The following day, Walter wrote to Rita. "It seems such a pity now that I have never had the pleasure of meeting you and of seeing my beloved skipper again."

Over the next couple of years, Mum tried a few ventures to make ends meet, such as turning the house into a convalescent home, a business which was not particularly well regulated in those days. Our first 'convalescent', a frail and elderly lady, fell out of bed and broke her hip soon after arriving, which quickly put an end to that idea. Then, at the age of 42, she got a job as a teaching assistant, and discovered her vocation. She went back to college, got a teaching diploma, and embarked on a successful teaching career, giving her a regular income and an occupation that she loved. She was finally in a position to buy her first little cottage, and was kept busy in her spare time stripping beams, ripping out fireplaces, and turning her hand to any work that needed to be done. By this time we were married with families of our own and, as we got older, we began to talk of Dad more often. We found that we had all retained slightly different memories, some of which were anecdotes from his time as a pilot, usually related to us by Mum. The burning of Tito's coat was a favourite, and we knew that a crew member had fallen from his plane, and that Dad had been with partisans in Poland, but we had no clear idea of the type of work he was doing. Why was he flying from Libya and Italy? We didn't really know. Then in 2011, my daughter Rachel did some research on the internet and found that journalist Paul Lashmar had taken an interest in the story, with a view to making a television documentary based on the Storey crew's final flight. When she eventually tracked him down he was living just a few miles away and, with great generosity, he gave us copies of his research material. This was the start. The information was intriguing and, by this time, I had also come across a book by Graham Pitchfork, 'Shot Down and on the Run', which contained a chapter on Dad's crew, and a book by Nina Mierzwinska-Harper, which told the same story but from the viewpoint of the Polish partisans. My interest was growing with every bit of information and I wanted to know more. I decided that the first step was to gather all the threads of information together into one cohesive narrative, and then fill in the gaps, if possible.

Greg Kusiak, Tarnogora 2013

I began my own research, and in the early stages much of this was on the internet. I posted questions on various websites, particularly with regard to the exact crash site of Halifax JP 224, but had little response. And then, out of the blue, I received a message from Greg Kusiak, a young man from the village of Letownia in southern Poland, just a few miles from the area where the Halifax came down. He had always taken a great interest in the historic event, and wrote offering to take a picture of the crash site for me. He did just that, but what I had not expected was that a memorial stone had been erected at the location, between the village of Tarnogora and the hamlet of Poreba, in the district of Nowa Sarzyna. The reason I had not expected it, was that nobody had died in the crash. The little monument, alone in a field on the edge of the village, was to commemorate the actions of brave partisans and villagers who had saved the lives of four British airmen in April 1944. At this point, the summer of 2012, Mum, my sisters and I decided to travel to Poland. Dad had written in his letter to Ali all those years ago: "I would really like to come to Poland and see you all, but unfortunately I am not a rich man, so I doubt if I can ever be able to do it". There seemed no reason why we couldn't go to Poland for him. So, on the 19th April, 2013, the four of us, 'the team', boarded a flight from Liverpool John Lennon Airport to Krakow, and then took a train to the town of Przeworsk. There we were met by Edward Kak, the man whose dedication and perseverance had seen the erection of the monument, and kept the story alive for the young people of Tarnogora.

Nothing could have prepared us for the welcome we received upon arrival. From the moment we arrived at the railway station we were looked after by Edward, his family, and the villagers of Tarnogora. We were introduced to mayors and schoolchildren alike, and taken on a tour of all the sites relevant to us, in the company of historian Piotr Galdys and ex-partisan Bronislaw Smola. We were invited to eat at the home of Bronislaw Sowa, who as a young man had run to get help for Tom Storey on that first night, and everywhere we went, someone came along to help with translation, transport, or to provide food for us. We were quite overwhelmed by the hospitality and the strong sense of community in Tarnogora. On the anniversary day, the 23rd April, we gathered at the Tarnogora primary school, where the children presented us with flowers and then danced, recited poetry, and sang for us. From the school, we walked to the monument, which was adorned with flags, and Rita unveiled a new plaque dedicated to the seven airmen on that ill-fated flight. Piotr Galdys presented Rita with the airman's flying helmet, which had been salvaged from the crashed Halifax by Sebastian Lyko almost seventy years earlier, and Edward Kak gave us each a piece of the salvaged wing section. It was a particularly emotional day for us as it was also the anniversary of Dad's death in 1964, and for all those years following his death we had struggled with the memory of his leaving us, and wanted,

Author with Edward Kak, Tarnogora 2013

above all else to understand why. We needed some peace of mind, and although we did not expect to find it in Tarnogora, that is exactly what happened.

We knew that the 23rd April was a significant anniversary for Dad because every year, on that date, he would withdraw completely from everything around him and seek some kind of oblivion. That led us to believe that the place he retreated to was a lonely and fearful place. It was the fire that began to open our minds to the truth – the fire lit by Piotr Galdys and Lukasz Kak in the forest close to Tarnogora. Having collected dry brushwood from the forest floor and got the fire alight, they pulled up clods of damp peat with their hands and brought them to surround the flames and contain them. Fresh twigs were then gathered, and sausages skewered on the end for us to cook on the fire. Bronislaw Smola talked of his days with the partisans, as Edward, Barbara and Joanna Kak carried baskets of food to the woodland camp. A bottle of vodka and a shot glass came out of one of the baskets, and many toasts were drunk. 'Na zdrowie!' (Cheers!). Fire meant something to Dad far beyond the need to keep warm, and suddenly we knew why – it was the fire of comradeship, purpose and the company of people who know the value of life, and were the best companions a man could have in his lifetime.

Back at our hotel, we sat in the lobby in semi-darkness and talked, and talked. We had all experienced something quite profound, and were very affected by it. We now realised that Tom had been in the company of people who were fighting for their lives and the freedom of their children, yet were able to extend the hand of friendship and care to an outsider, who could offer them nothing, and whose very existence brought the prospect of death to them and their families. We had all experienced a complete reversal of our previous thoughts. He did not look back on this as a scene from a nightmare, but as a brief period in his life when his fate was in the hands of people who not only kept him safe, a complete stranger, but valued his attempt to bring them help when all around them was abandonment and betrayal. He offered to fight alongside them, and the offer was genuine because he felt as though he belonged and was part of the struggle himself. We felt quite stunned by this sudden realisation, which had not come from my detailed research, or even from first-hand crew accounts. It had come from our own communion with the families who, seventy years earlier, had offered a lifeline to Tom and his crew: Kida, Kak, Galdys, Smola, Wolcz, Sowa, and many more. It was these same families and the community of Tarnogora who were extending the hand of unreserved friendship down the generations to us, and we were humbled by it.

I have read many accounts of the hardship and privations endured by the airmen in the forest, and all of it is true. Tom came down on the outskirts of Tarnogora injured, in pain, and in shock. The trauma of that night lived with him in nightmares for many months once he reached the safety of home, but he had been in the care of good people who looked after him, helped his fellow crew members, and provided an escape route where none seemed possible. I now think that when he sought oblivion on that date, it was not to escape his time in the Polish forest, but to escape his life in the present – the vacuous life of a commercial traveller for a soft drinks company, followed by unemployment, and the loss of purpose, direction, and self-esteem. He was a clever, funny, lovely man who, at the age of 24 had experienced an extraordinary level of fear, self-doubt, loyalty, pride, and love, and it changed him.

He could never settle back into the life that was pre-ordained for a working-class grammar-school boy. Oddly enough, that gives me peace of mind and a sense of closure, because I know that although he could have lived a longer life, he lived a very full and complete life. I am happy for him that he achieved so much. *Per Adua Ad Astra* – through the clouds to the stars – that is exactly what you did, Dad.x

AND FINALLY

Looking back to my 'Introduction', written more than a year ago, I see that I wrote, with great naivety "I believe the truth is in the facts", and I am embarrassed by those words with the benefit of hindsight. I will not rewrite them though, because this is a record of my own personal journey and I genuinely believed that statement when I committed it to paper. Of course I now realise that, unless I was a witness myself to the events I have described in this book, the facts are simply a framework on top of which I have built layer upon layer of interpretation – my own interpretation! I started out in the belief that the key to understanding my father lay somewhere within his two tours of duty with 148 Squadron, and his subsequent months spent with partisans, and I expected to find courage, heroism, and sacrifice. In the end, what I found was a quiet integrity. I have been reduced to tears by accounts of young men and women who were faced with the most unimaginable circumstances, and yet retained their humanity and dignity. And it crosses boundaries. The German officers who accompanied Eddie and Hap to Dulag Luft, protecting them from reprisals on the journey, and buying them a beer at some desolate railway station on the way. Stanislaw Belzynski, family man and academic, who committed himself to the resistance and was shot by Germans two weeks after escorting four British men to safety over the River San. Wing Commander James Blackburn, who led his men in the air by example, and then sat up until the early hours of the morning catching up on paperwork. Feliks and Catherine Sitarz, who provided food and human kindness to desperate people waiting to cross the River San. Mr and Mrs Dec, who became a mother and father to Walter Davis, risking the lives of their entire family in their determination to keep him safe. Vladimir Pavlov, pilot of a Soviet Dakota, admired and respected by all who knew him, and yet he regarded himself as no better than any other member of the crew. He risked everything to get his overladen aircraft off the ground rather than leave any of the injured or desperate passengers behind. And lastly, there was Nina, who began her partisan training at the age of eleven, and confidently guided grown men, soldiers, through treacherous terrain, and carried messages between Polish and Russian partisan units.

The crew of Halifax JP224 never considered themselves heroes, and would have been embarrassed by such a description, and yet there is something about their youthful exuberance and steely determination to do the job they were given knowing that they could perish in the attempt, that is very touching. They obeyed orders and followed the correct procedures, even when things went horribly wrong, and they did not come out of it unscathed. Their experience as evaders took a toll on their long-term health and wellbeing and yet, it is my belief that whatever hardship they endured, nothing affected them more than the loss of Peter Crosland in November 1943. Following the tragedy, they climbed back into their aircraft and continued to carry out their duty, while overwhelmed by loss and sadness and that quiet kind of courage has, at the end of my search, moved me the most. Tom Storey returned from the war, as he had joined it, without a trace of bitterness, and with his gentle nature and integrity intact. What he did lose was his peace of mind, and in telling this story, I feel that I have found the place he retreated to in the flickering flames. It was a place of strong friendship, good people, and a sense of purpose. Words written by John

Mulgan shortly before he died in 1944 struck a chord with me when I first read them, and they continue to resonate now:

"In war, when you are working well together, you find the sober pleasure of working in concert with friends and companions and at the same time feel pride in yourself for the part which you can play as an individual. I believe this fact to be one reason why men are happy in wartime. Honest men know that war is to be fought and destroyed for the suffering and pain and crime that go with it. But honest men will also admit that they themselves as individuals have been happy in wartime, and some of them have afterwards tried to find the same thing in peace and always failed."[i]

Tom Storey aged 16 (team player) with Carlisle Grammar School Cricket XI 1936
(Photo courtesy of Trinity School, Carlisle)

The life you love is the life worth living
To love your life is a gift worth giving
If life is not love, the fire has gone out
Return to the spark where love shone out.

(Susan Storey Hayhurst, May 2013)

The 'fire of friendship' 2013

AFTERWORD

" $\mathbf{A}$ nd now, set Europe ablaze", said Prime Minister Winston Churchill to Hugh Dalton, Minister of Economic Warfare. This quotation has come to be seen as Churchill's command to found the Special Operations Executive, whose role was "to coordinate all action, by way of subversion and sabotage, against the enemy overseas". It was July 1940.

In order to facilitate the execution of the War Cabinet plans, anti-German resistance movements had to be equipped with explosives, grenades, land mines, detonators, rockets, ammunition, automatic firearms and radio sets. Without such supplies, destroying German trains, committing acts of subversion and training volunteers to attack the enemy rearguard after the opening of the second front, thus supporting the Allied troop landings, would have been very difficult.

Let us fast forward to 1943. All across Europe, resistance fighters from every occupied nation, looked to British Liberator and Halifax aircraft to deliver them supplies and support; Italian partisans, resistance fighters following orders from the Danish Freedom Council, "Jossings" from the Norwegian Milorg movement and Greek combatants from ELAS[1]. A hopeful look to the sky was also cast by the People's Liberation

---

[1] ELAS (the Greek People's Liberation Army)

Army in Yugoslavia, fighting against German forces in the mountains of Bosnia and Herzegovina. The same feeling of expectation was aroused in Dutch patriots who planned sabotage in the occupied Netherlands as well as their friends from the Belgian National Movement, the French *maquis* and troops of the Home Army in occupied Poland. Tom Storey and his crew were on the front line of this dangerous and important delivery service without really being exposed to the real war on the ground. That is until Sunday 23rd April 1944 when engine failure meant that the crew were propelled into the world of the resistance fighters. They baled out of their plane on Sunday, 23 April 1944 and, having touched down somewhere in Poland, the crew of Halifax JP224 embarked on a whole new experience of "World War II".

The names of all the Polish people who helped others during the period of German and Soviet occupation have not been written down to this day. It would take a legion of researchers. The only organisation that tracks such figures is the Yad Vashem Institute in Jerusalem, which has been collecting names for years. The institute also awards the title of "Righteous Among the Nations" to those who brought help to the Jews in World War II. Half of the people honoured are Polish. There is no such list of patriots involved in hiding, providing false papers, freeing from prisoner-of-war camps or helping evaders from Great Britain, Canada, the United States of America or Australia but if such a list existed, it would include the two girl scouts killed for providing assistance to British captives. They were: Janina Lechówa, beheaded at the Cytadela in Poznań and Janina Olszewska, shot dead together with her father by a firing squad in her home village in Lipno County. Two other women, Zofia Garlicka, 68 years old, and her daughter Zofia Jasińska were sent to Auschwitz for providing medical treatment to escaped British officers. Olga Kamińska-Prokopowa was beheaded for helping the British, Józef Grabiński and Wiesława Jezierska were executed following an investigation.

In April 1942, Ludwik Bayer, who had been hiding a runaway British officer, was hanged from a pear tree in his own garden in the village of Dymarczewo Stare near Poznań. Three Poles: Józef Hanasz, Robert Hatko and Teodor Tom were hanged on 18 November 1941 in Brzozowice-Kamień; they helped hide and showed the way to a captive who had escaped from a camp in Łambinowice. On 28 November 1943 a Home Army patrol transporting a group of runaway British captives was attacked by gendarmes. The airmen were saved but in revenge, the Germans killed 42 residents of Bichniów. Maria Eugenia Jasińska, a pharmacist, was hanged in Lodz on 20 April 1943 for providing aid to British pilots. Her family received "words of appreciation" from the RAF. The Polish government showed their appreciation by awarding the Silver Cross of the Virtuti Militari War Order, Poland's highest military decoration.

Thomas Storey and four of his crew from Halifax JP 224 were not taken prisoner. Despite having landed in a German training area they evaded capture thanks to the actions of these admirable people. Only two of the crew fell into enemy hands; the other five were saved. Walter Davies, sheltering in Smolarzyny near Rakszawa, lived to see the arrival of Allied Soviet forces. Storey, Keen, Hughes and Stradling, hidden by partisans of the Peasants' Battalions and the Home Army, were transferred across the San River to the partisan unit led by Franciszek Przysiężniak – "Father Jan", and were eventually taken to a Polish-Soviet detachment headed by Mikołaj Kunicki – "Mucha". One night two aircraft arrived from Kiev at a prepared landing ground. The wounded partisans and the four airmen boarded those planes and flew out.

In 1996, when I was writing the "Last Flight of the Halifax" book, together with Jerzy Piekarczyk, we met several soldiers who had been involved in the clandestine rescue; they were simply obeying orders to help the Allies wage war against

Hitler. We also came across people who were not involved with the partisan movement, yet they still put their families' and their own lives at risk because... it was the right thing to do; these airmen had provided our boys with ammunition and equipment. Once the aircrew had joined a partisan group, they could not subsequently decide to give themselves up to the enemy because of the information they held, which could be tortured out of them by the Germans. This was how the German Special Court got their proof and imposed capital punishment on Irena Markiewiczowa, Bronisław Sobkowiak, Maria Klichowska, Bolesław Kierczyński, Bernard Drozd, Witold Wiktor Łaszczyński and Michalina Gorczycowa, who were all beheaded on 15 December 1942. The two young offenders: Klara Dolniak and Zbigniew Klichowski were sent to a concentration camp.

I bow my head in respect of the brave pilots and crews of 334 Special Duty Wing, whilst recognizing that the names of Polish underground and people who just helped them, will never be fully known and cannot be thanked.

Stanisław Maria Jankowski

APPENDIX 1

Transcript of message sent 21ˢᵗ June 1944 from British Military Mission Moscow to Mediterranean Allied Air Force Headquarters

To: H.Q.
M.A.A.F.
From: 30 Mission
AIR.531
21 June 1944

Further my following report Flight Engineer Halifax JP 224. Begins

"At approx. 23.30 B on 23 April whilst on an operational flight and descending from 13,000 feet over the CARPATHIAN MOUNTAINS the oil temperature on the P.I. engine began to rise quickly and the pressure dropped 10 lbs. When the temperature reached 80 degrees the captain feathered the engine. Six minutes later the captain reported the S.I. engine had suddenly cut, just after having changed fuel tanks from 2 & 4 to 1 & 3. The fuel warning light did not show. I immediately changed back to tank No. 2 and efforts were made to re-start the P.I. engine but it refused the start. There was no warning that the engine was about to stop, such as spluttering, swing or fluctuating boost, but it cut dead. My gauges for this engine also gave no indication of an impending stoppage. There were still 1500 gallons of fuel left which could not be jettisoned and the aircraft would not keep height on 2 engines.

(Sgd) J. Keen, Sgt Flight Engineer".

Letter signed by Flight Lieutenant ....Win...........(unreadable)

Author's Note:

The accounts of that final flight vary from one crewmember to another and the issue of which engines failed is the most significant. Tom Storey, during debriefing, stated that the port inner engine overheated and was shut down and then the port outer engine stopped dead. Charlie Keen, in his own debrief, stated that the second engine to cut was the starboard inner. Some of the crew also stated that a third engine began to fail. Because of these discrepancies, I have stuck to the account given by the pilot, Tom Storey, who would have been acutely aware of an engine failure because of the handling properties that it imposed on him. A 100% accurate account is probably not possible now.

APPENDIX 2

Letter written by Tom Storey to Alojzego Pajaka 1945

Dear Alojzy,

I got your address from the Polish Red Cross. I am sorry to hear that after I left Poland you were taken into captivity. Still, you should consider yourself lucky that you survived, as you know they used to hang partisans. I obviously just got out with my life as the Germans shot at the Russian plane.

Remember Urech (or George as we used to call him) singing 'Moja Malgorzato' and how much he was longing for his wife at that time. I often sing the partisan songs which you guys taught me. I have not forgotten any of them. After I got back, I didn't rejoin the war against the enemy. As you know, I was fighting for a long time and because of my experience I got a job as a test pilot.

I have met Mr. Mycholichnik (sorry I can't write his name properly) your Prime Minister of the Polish Government in London – I know he is in Poland now.

Three members of my crew, who were captured by Germans, fortunately made it back here. They were treated very badly by the Germans. A lot of my friends from the Squadron were killed delivering supplies to Warsaw. We did everything possible for your country but unfortunately the obstacles were too great. Whatever you think of politicians, positive or negative, remember one thing Ali, those English boys gave their lives to help their friends. We are also very grateful to you and thousands of other partisans for your fight during these darkest of days.

Please tell all comrades that I would be very happy to hear from them. Could you ask them to send me their photograph because I can't remember all the names – only the nicknames

I would really like to come to Poland and see you all but unfortunately I am not a rich man so I doubt if I can ever be able to do it.

I have to say thank you to you and your comrades for all the happy moments we shared, despite being constantly under threat from the Germans.

Signed Tom Storey

APPENDIX 3

Transcript of a letter written by Tom Storey to Stanislaw Mikolajczyk in November 1947

Unicorn Hotel
Corve Street
Ludlow
Salop

4 – 11 – 47

Dear Mr Mikolajczyk,

I wish to offer my congratulations to you on your escape from Poland. I also sympathise with you for having to escape twice from your own country in the space of a few years.

Perhaps you will remember me as the RAF pilot who was shot down in Poland and lived for a while with your partisans. On my escape to this country I was ordered up to London to meet you at the Polish Embassy and at the same time I met the Polish C in C.

Being an escaper from enemy territory myself I can understand the mental and physical strain you have undergone, and I am happy that you have sought refuge in this country as I did with your people.

I have recently written an article which has been accepted for publication in the near future, on what I know of Russia, in the hope that is will put this country on guard against them and also help Poland and other occupied countries in their struggle for freedom.

I trust a good rest will be granted you and I reiterate I am glad you got away. If I could be of any help to you at all I would be happy to try to reciprocate your kindness to me.

I am, Sir,
Your obedient servant

Signed T. Storey

APPENDIX 4

Chapter 1:

Crew of Halifax JN888 of 148 Squadron, lost 26th November 1943
Sgt Peter Crosland RAFVR

Crew of Halifax EB140 of 624 Squadron, lost 1st December 1943
F/Sgt Dennis John Howlett RAFVR
F/Sgt Raymond Percival Atkinson RAFVR
Cpl Sidney George Cleland RAFVR
F/Sgt Arthur Ernest Edwards RAFVR
F/Sgt John Kenneth Hughes RAFVR
F/Sgt Vernon Leslie Miller RCAF
F/Sgt James Kenneth Shewring RAFVR

SOE Mission Personnel, lost 1st December 1943
Major Ian Smart
Captain Jack Stephenson
Lieutenant Alan Toley
George McKenna
Corporal Ian Kesterton

Crew of Liberator AL509 of 148 Squadron, lost 3rd December 1943
F/Lt Maurice Passmore RAFVR
WO James Herbert Stevenson Clarke RCAF

F/Lt Eldon Burke Elliott RCAF
F/Lt Harry James Crawford RNZAF
F/Sgt Edwin Archibald Toole RCAF
WO Ralph Edward Hawken RCAF
F/Sgt William Joseph Dowle RAFVR

Chapter 2:

Crew of Halifax JN888 of 624 Squadron, lost 14ᵗʰ July 1944
P/O Leslie Arthur Peers RCAF
F/O Albert John Baythorp RAFVR
Sgt Jack Brooke RAFVR
Sgt Harry Clarke RAFVR
F/O Charles Spencer Goble RAFVR
Sgt James Edward Walsh RAFVR
Sgt William Ronald Wharmby RAFVR

Crew of Halifax HR674 of 148 Squadron, lost 19ᵗʰ October 1943
F/Lt William Ross Forester RAFVR
F/Sgt James Clement Cole RAFVR
F/O Peter Raymond Flyte RAFVR
F/O Francis Jack Hunter RNZAF
F/O Edward Frank Myers RAFVR
Sgt Peter Twiddy RAFVR
F/Sgt Harold Williams RAFVR

SOE Personnel lost 19ᵗʰ October 1943
Captain Alfred Careless RAC
Signalman David William Rockingham RCS

Chapter 3:

SOE SPILLWAY mission personnel lost 1ˢᵗ February 1944
Major G.E. Layzell, South Lancashire Regiment

Crew of Halifax JN959 of 148 Squadron, lost 11th February 1944

F/Sgt Ian McGugan RAAF
F/Sgt Bernard Austin Hough RAAF
F/Sgt Percy Garfield Mann RAAF
F/Sgt Edward George Lee RAAF
F/Sgt Nairne Edwin Plaxton DFM RAF
Sgt James Palmer RAFVR
Sgt Frederick Moses Cyril Henry Harris RAFVR

Crew of Halifax JP292 of 148 Squadron, lost 3/4 July 1944

W/O Charles Thomas Fairweather RAF
F/O John Stanley Brown RCAF
F/Sgt John Easton RAFVR
P/O Allen Haigh RAFVR
F/Sgt Ronald Frederick Houghton RAFVR
F/Sgt Richard Jacques RAFVR
F/Sgt Leonard James Smith RAFVR

Crew of Halifax JP286 of 148 Squadron lost 3/4 July 1944

Sqdn Ldr Surray Philip Victor Bird RAFVR
F/O Kenneth Peter Mcleod Cran RAFVR
F/Sgt Peter Lake RAFVR
F/Sgt Arthur Archer Lee RAFVR
P/O Harold Pearson RAF
F/Sgt Ronald Radford RAFVR
W/O Donal David Charles Stewart RCAF
F/Sgt Marcel Tilmont RAFVR

SOE personnel lost December 1944

2nd Lt Alexander Francis Vass
Major Richard Moncrieff Wright R.T.R

Crew of Halifax JP247 of 148 Squadron lost 3/4 July 1944

F/Lt George Raymond Wood RAFVR
F/Sgt James William Hern RAF

Crew of Halifax JP179 of 148 Squadron lost 3/5 July 1944
F/Sgt Evan Ffoulkes Jones RAFVR
F/Sgt John Kennedy RAF
W/O John Phillip Harrison RAFVR
Sgt Thomas William Hugh Tomlinson RAFVR

SOE MULLIGATAWNY mission personnel lost March-July 1944
Maj Mostyn Davies
Sgt J. Walker
Sgt N. Munro
Cpl J.R. Shannon
Sig R.G. Watts

SOE CLARIDGE mission personnel lost July 1944
Maj W.F. Thompson

Crew of Halifax BB444 of 624 Squadron lost 1st February 1944
F/Sgt E.D.S. Tennant RAAF
F/O Stanley RAFVR
Sgt J.L. Devine RAFVR
F/Sgt D.H. Potter RAAF
Sgt F.C.R. Burlefinger RAFVR
Sgt G.Gardner RAFVR

Chapter 4:

Crew of Halifax HR660 of 148 Squadron, lost 3rd March, 1944
F/Lt James Harold Botham RAFVR
F/Sgt John Walter Sole RAFVR
W/O John Caldwell Calhoun RCAF
F/O Henry George Lancaster RAFVR
Sgt William Ernest Thurnall RAFVR

Chapter 8:

Crew of Halifax JP162 of 148 Squadron, lost 4/5 August, 1944
F/Lt James Girvan McCall RAFVR
Sgt Clifford Aspinall RAFVR
Sgt John Frederick Cairney Rae RAFVR

APPENDIX 5

The following crewmembers flew at least one operational sortie with the Storey crew:

F/Sgt T. Storey	Pilot
F/Sgt E. Elkington-Smith	Bomb Aimer
W/O O.W. Congdon	Navigator
Sgt W. G. Davis	Wireless Operator
Sgt C.J. Keen	Flight Engineer
Sgt J.C. Hughes	Rear Gunner
Sgt P. Stradling	Despatcher
Sgt P. Crosland	Bomb Aimer
F/O W.W. Nichol	Navigator
Sgt G. Fidler	Despatcher
Sgt W. Woolliscroft	Flight Engineer
LAC Martin	Flight Engineer
Sgt N.A. Robertson	Bomb Aimer
Sgt T.R. Lawman	Navigator
Sgt H.W. Humphreys	not known
Sgt D. H. Crockford	Navigator
F/O W.A.Fullar	Bomb Aimer
Sgt W.M. Tilton	not known
F/O H. O'Neill	not known
F/Sgt R. Chapman	not known
Sgt M. Tilmont	Rear Gunner
F/Sgt R. Lee	Navigator

The crew flew almost all their early sorties in Halifax JN888, the aircraft they had flown to North Africa from the United Kingdom. They personalised the nose of this aircraft with artwork and the name RITA. After the move to Brindisi in January 1944, they flew a variety of aircraft, including JN888, until she went to Algeria for an engine change at the end of March 1944. The following is a list of aircraft flown by the Storey crew with 148 Squadron:

JN888
BB445
JN925
JN896
BB381
BB318
HR671
BB431
BB338
JP224 (final flight)

ACKNOWLEDGEMENTS

I owe a huge debt of gratitude to Eddie Elkington-Smith, Second Pilot and Navigator, for the written accounts and logbook pages which he gave to the family and to Charles Keen, Flight Engineer, who travelled from Brighton to Lancaster in 2003 to talk to my family about the crew and their time with 148 Special Duty Squadron. Wireless Operator Walter Davis, who I had the privilege to meet in 2013, his daughter Anne Black and granddaughter Sharon Spencer contributed a wealth of interesting material to my project, including a memoir, photographs, M.I.9 Reports and access to Walter's Flying logbook. Mike Bedford-Stradling, son of Patrick Stradling, Air Gunner and Despatcher, has been enormously helpful and generous with his father's archive of material and lastly my mother, Rita, who preserved letters, photographs and memories over the years, which have been of great value to me.

Whilst researching the material for this book, I found my way to the Operation Dark of the Moon website, which was set up by Terry Maker for the research of 148 Squadron, and other Special Duty Squadrons, during the Second World War. Members of this forum have provided me with material, given me an insight into the activities of the Squadron and perhaps most of all, provided tremendous support and encouragement. In particular I would like to mention Terry Maker, Steve Andrews, Bill Pogson, Rosemary Edmeads, Steve Alves, Adriano Silva Baumgartner, Julie Fairweather, Pat Atkins,

Kleon Ionnidis, Steven Horsfield, Piotr Hodyra and Larry Toft. Larry has been guide and mentor to me throughout the process of this book and his familiarity with the technique of flying a Halifax and knowledge of 148 Squadron has given authenticity to the flight sections. His wealth of experience as a World War II Special Duty Pilot has been both practically invaluable and emotionally inspirational. Rosemary Edmeads and I have been on a parallel course with our writing projects and she has supported and helped me unreservedly. Don Kaiser was particularly helpful when I needed an authentic photograph of the 1944 eruption of Vesuvius and allowed me to use one from his website. A further source of invaluable information has been the Carpetbagger Aviation Museum and in particular the database of Aircraft lost on Allied Force's Special Duty Operations & Associated Roll of Honour kept and updated by Roy Tebbutt.

I must thank The National Archives at Kew for providing such an excellent research facility. Some of the most productive and enjoyable days were spent in the Reader's room, at a comfortable desk by the window, working my way through files. The joy of finding a piece of paper linking one of my father's flights to the SOE personnel he carried, cannot be described. The research process opened my eyes to the amount of work that goes into producing a factual, historical account and my gratitude to the authors of some of the books I relied on heavily, is boundless. In some cases, the books provided 'scene-setting' information or historical context and in other cases, very specific information which allowed me to make the link between operations in the air and groups on the ground. I met Graham Pitchfork, author of Shot Down and on the Run shortly before I began to write this story and found his book invaluable and his enthusiasm motivational to the point that I wanted to do something myself. I am also particularly grateful to David Stafford for responding to my plea for information on Italian drop zones and to Richard Clogg for information on the Allied Military Mission in Greece. Jonathan Walker gave me very useful information on the Polish Resistance Groups and Alan Ogden steered me towards some relevant TNA files and also gave me sound advice on taking photographs of the pages after my disastrous first attempts. Roderick Bailey, whose book The Wildest Province became a 'bible' for me when writing about Albanian Operations not only helped enormously but was very supportive at a time when I needed it! Towards the end of this project, I was delighted to be able to make contact with Stanislaw Jankowski, author of Ostatni Lot Halifaxa, the definitive work on the loss of Halifax JP224, and he not only offered to check my 'Polish' Chapters for me, which has given me great peace of mind, but wrote an Afterword for this book. I am immensely grateful to him and the authors of the above-mentioned books who took the time to help me.

I found the Air Historical Branch of the RAF particularly helpful and I would like to thank Mike Hatch and Flight Lieutenant Hudson for taking the time to find specific information which was important for my story. Irena Czernichowska of Stanford University Hoover Institute managed to find a letter my father had written to Stanislaw Mikolajczyk in 1947 amongst the Mikolajczyk papers, held by the Institute and I am very grateful to her for that. Svetlana Kostyleva, also of Stanford, copied the diary of Brigadier Hill for me and Grzyna Wadas of the Bibliotek, Nowa Sarzyna provided me with archive material pertaining to the Halifax crash. Thank you Alison McCulloch of Carlisle Grammar School for not only unearthing Tom Storey's school report with its credit in 'German', but also for finding a photograph of young Tom in the School Cricket Team! Greg Kusiak managed to pinpoint for me the exact spot where Halifax JP224 crashed and also gave me links to a Polish television documentary based on the last flight of this aircraft, all of which enabled me to 'home in' on the relevant area to research. It was Greg who put me in touch with Edward Kak from the village of Tarnogora, which resulted in our visit there in 2013. I would also like to thank Dawid Sowa for alerting me to the fact that a diary existed, written by Bronislaw Kaminski, detailing events as they happened on the ground at the time of the Halifax crash. Pawel Cholewa, the grandson of Kaminski, subsequently copied all the relevant pages for me and I am immensely grateful for that priceless information. Thanks also to Jakub Kędzior, Project Manager of the VeroLing Agency for translating those thirty five handwritten pages so perfectly and to Renata Elgalal for assistance with Polish documents.

For having the patience to read through early chapters of this book and coming up with excellent suggestions I would like to thank Polly Morland, Peter Gwillim, Charles Morland and Mike Bedford-Stradling and for checking every chapter, as the book developed, I can only say sincere and heartfelt thanks to Wayne Elkin and Larry Toft. Wayne read every word with painstaking care and kept the story grounded by curbing my 'flights of fancy' and Larry took the same care with the flying sequences, making sure that I presented those aspects of the story as accurately as possible. I would also like to thank Nicholas Morland, who advised on flying matters and provided me with a copy of Pilot and Flight Engineer's Notes for the Halifax. My sisters, Pat Bowskill and Susan Hayhurst have consistently helped by jogging my memory and adding anecdotes of their own and my mother, Rita has been extremely generous with her time and support.

When it came to checking the final manuscript, I was very grateful to Andrea and Terry Reeves, for reading it through, picking up inconsistencies and making suggestions. I received my first 'review' from Andrea and will not forget her thoughtful and generous words. Both Terry and Andrea have given me invaluable advice throughout the process of this work, particularly when it came to the minefield of self-publishing. Jo Ashley was a great help during the final pre-publishing week by doing a last read-through for me and lastly, two people I trust implicitly with my work are my daughters, Rachel Arey and Maxine Morland. They have worked their way through the manuscript for me; Rachel to advise on final presentation and Maxine to do the professional job of editing and copy proofing. They have been an incredible source of inspiration for me and I consider myself very lucky to have had such unstinting support and practical help.

Our trip to Poland in April 2013 was the highlight of this project and for the welcome we received and the hospitality offered I would like to thank Edward, Barbara, Joanna and Lukasz Kak, Tadeusz and Zofia Kak, Piotr and Margaret Kak, Greg Kusiak, Piotr Galdys, Bronislaw Smola, Damien Majkut, Bronislaw Sowa, Jan Kido, Jerzy Paul, Danuta Pinderska, Violetta Fimiarz and the staff and pupils of Tarnogora Primary School.

Lastly I must thank Paul Lashmar who not only provided me with copies of his own research, but continued to advise and support me throughout the process of writing this book. A busy journalist, lecturer and film maker, he made the time to help me and I am very grateful for that.

NOTES

Chapter 1

[i] Cypher message 8th Oct 1943, Cairo to MONKEYWRENCH, WO202/331.
[ii] Cypher message 10th Oct 1943, Cairo to MONKEYWRENCH, WO202/331.
[iii] Cypher message 21st Oct 1943, MONKEYWRENCH to Cairo, WO202/331.
[iv] **Our Man in Yugoslavia,** Sebastian Ritchie, Frank Cass Publishers 2004, pages 68 & 75.
[v] **My Grandad's Story,** Walter Davis and Sharon Spencer, 2007 personal recollections.
[vi] **The Wildest Province** by Roderick Bailey, Vintage 2009. Reproduced by permission of The Random House Group Limited, page 225.
[vii] Insight on this particular incident provided by Larry Toft, of 148 Squadron.
[viii] **Illyrian Adventure,** Brigadier 'Trotsky' Davies, Bodley Head, 1952, Page 70.
[ix] Report by Major McAdam on activities 16th May 1943-19th November 1944, HS5/692.
[x] Recorded account by Charles Keen 2003.
[xi] Recorded account by Charles Keen 2003.
[xii] Storey family letter archive.
[xiii] Information on the loss of Peter Crosland taken from squadron records and information supplied by Flight Lieutenant M. Hudson of the Air Historical Branch (RAF) in personal correspondence.
[xiv] **My Grandad's Story,** Walter Davis and Sharon Spencer 2007, personal recollections.
[xv] ORB Appendices November 1943 page 37, AIR27/998.
[xvi] Speech to the House of Commons 22nd February, 1944.

Special Note:
Unless otherwise stated, all flight and crew information was sourced from:

148 Operations Record Book, October & November 1943, AIR27/995.
148 Sortie Reports (RAF form 441A), AIR23/1443.

Additional information on operations and Squadron activities sourced from:

148 Operations Record Book Summary, October & November 1943, AIR27/995.

Information on lost aircraft and crews either sourced or confirmed with the help of:

Harrington Aviation Museum Society. Listing of Allied aircraft lost on Special Duty Operations. www.harringtonmuseum.org.uk.

Much of the piecing together of the Albania supply and personnel drops was done with the help of Roderick Bailey's Book, **The Wildest Province,** Vintage 2009 (reproduced by permission of The Random House Group Limited) in conjunction with 148 operational records as mentioned above. I have not marked every source individually. Suffice to say, I could not have matched personnel with specific flights without the help of this particular book. I have also been grateful to Walter Davis and Sharon Spencer for allowing me to use the personal recollections of Walter Davis.

Chapter 2

[i.] **Operation Autonomous,** Ivor Porter, Chatto & Windus 1989, Chapter 11.
[ii.] **Operation Autonomous,** Ivor Porter, Chatto & Windus 1989, Chapter 11.
[iii.] **Through Hitler's Back Door,** Alan Ogden, Pen & Sword Books 2010, pages 249-63.
[iv.] **Operation Autonomous,** Ivor Porter, Chatto & Windus, Page 102.
[v.] RAF form 441A AIR49/223.
[vi.] Recorded account by Charles Keen, 2003.
[vii.] Conditions in Zervas-held territory in Greece by D.J. Wallace, **British Reports on Greece 1943-44.**
[viii.] Report of activities in Greece, T/Sgt Spiros Kaleyias, HS5/697.
[ix.] **Venture into Greece,** Nicholas Hammond DSO, William Kimber, 1983, chapter 8.
[x.] Robert E. Moyers: OSS dentist with the Greek resistance, Jonathan D Clemente MD, **OSS Society Journal**
[xi.] **Illyrian Venture,** Brigadier 'Trotsky' Davies, Bodley Head, 1952, page 97.
[xii.] **When Men and Mountains Meet,** H.W. Tilman, D.S.O, M.C., Cambridge University Press 1946
[xiii.] 148 Squadron RAF reports 43-45 (medical reports), AIR49/996.
[xiv.] Signal MONKEYWRENCH to Cairo, 10th October 1943, WO202/331.

[xv.] Signal MONKEYWRENCH to Cairo, 1ˢᵗ March 1944, WO202/331

[xvi.] Signal Cairo to MONKEYWRENCH, 9ᵗʰ November 1943, WO202/331.

[xvii.] **Illyrian Adventure,** Brigadier 'Trotsky' Davies, Bodley Head, 1952, page 89.

[xviii.] 148 Squadron RAF reports 43-45 (medical reports), AIR49/996.

[xix.] **My Grandad's Story,** Walter Davis and Sharon Black, unpublished personal document.

[xx.] 148 Squadron RAF reports 43-45 (medical reports), AIR49/996.

[xxi.] Stradling family archive.

[xxii.] **Illyrian Adventure,** Brigadier Trotsky Davies, Bodley Head, 1952.

[xxiii.] Major J. Field, report, 1943, TNA HS 5/124, taken from **The Wildest Province**, Roderick Bailey, 2009, pages 195-196.

[xxiv.] Stradling family archive.

Special Note:
Unless otherwise stated, all flight and crew information was sourced from:

148 Operations Record Book, December 1943, AIR27/995.
148 Sortie Reports, December 1943 (RAF form 441A), AIR23/1443.

Additional information on operations and Squadron activities from:

148 Operations Record Book Summary, December 1943, AIR27/995.

Information on lost aircraft and crews either sourced or confirmed with the help of:

Harrington Aviation Museum Society. Listing of Allied aircraft Lost on Special Duty Operations. www.harringtonmuseum.org.uk.

Chapter 3

[i.] Personal correspondence from Adriano Silva Baumgartner to author.

[ii.] **Flights of the Forgotten,** Ken Merrick, 1989 Arms & Armour, page 178.

[iii.] **Through Hitler's Back Door,** Alan Ogden, 2010, page 141.

[iv.] ORB 624 Squadron, January 1944, AIR27/2142.

[v.] **Through Hitler's Back Door,** Alan Ogden, 2010, page 47.

[vi.] Personal communication Terry Maker, Dark of the Moon website to author.

[vii.] **Missing Believe Killed,** Article by Terry Maker, Dark of the Moon website.

[viii.] Information taken from Aircrew Remembered website, compiled by Terry Maker.

[ix] Reminiscence of Jack Pogson, via Dark of the Moon Website (Terry Maker).

[x] AIR27/999 F540, Appendixes E-I.

[xi] **Eastern Approaches,** Fitzroy Maclean, Penguin Books, 1991, page 413, and personal recollection of Jim Rosebottom, website: www.624squadron.

[xii] Telegram IN Rowena to Cairo 23/1 & 12/2, WO202/399.

[xiii] **Eastern Approaches,** Fitzroy Maclean, Penguin Books, 1991, page 432.

[xiv] **Partisan Picture,** Basil Davidson, Bedford Books 1946, page 196.

[xv] From the diary of Captain John Hibberdine, taken from **The Wildest Province**, Roderick Bailey, Vintage 2009, page 183.

[xvi] **Ostatni Lot Halifaxa,** Stanislaw M. Jankowski & Jerzy Piekarczyk, Oficyna Cracovia, 1997.

[xvii] RAAF Fatalities in WWII among Personnel serving in RAF Squadrons and Support Units (Alan Storr) website www.awm.gov.au.

[xviii] Appendix E to Report by Lt. Col. T.N.S. Wheeler, June 1944, HS5/127, and, **The Wildest Province,** Roderick Bailey, Vintage Books, 2009, reproduced by permission of The Random House Group Limited, page 231.

[xix] Interview with E. Elkington-Smith conducted by James Oliver for Paul Lashmar, February 1996.

[xx] Stradling family archive.

Special Note:
Unless otherwise stated, all flight and crew information was sourced from:

148 Operations Record Book, January & February 1944, AIR27/996.
148 Sortie Reports (RAF Form 441A), AIR23/1443.

Additional information on operations and Squadron activities from:

148 Operations Record Book Summary, January & February 1944, AIR27/996.

Information on lost aircraft and crews either sourced or confirmed with the help of:

Harrington Aviation Museum Society. Listing of Allied aircraft lost on Special Duty Operations. www.harringtonmuseum.org.uk.

Chapter 4

[i.] WO202/400 Savanna telegrams, February 1943.

[ii.] HS5/692 Appendix G to final report 6 Dec 44

[iii.] **My Grandad's Story,** Walter Davis and Sharon Black 2007, personal recollections.

[iv.] Personal correspondence fromAlan Ogden to author, 30th August 2012

[v.] **Report on Experience,** John Mulgan, Frontline Books 2010, page 126.

[vi.] Report on Italian Operations, 9th March 1944, AIR27/999.

[vii.] Interview with Eddie Elkington-Smith 1996 by James A. Oliver for Paul Lashmar.

[viii.] **The Central Blue,** Air Marshal Sir John Slessor, Cassell & Company, 1956.

[ix.] Don Kaiser, www.warwingsart.com/12thAirForce/Vesuvius.html

[x.] Recorded account by Charles Keen, 2003.

[xi.] **Partisan Picture,** Basil Davidson, Bedford Books, 1946, page 186.

[xii.] **Partisan Picture,** Basil Davidson, Bedford Books, 1946, page 191.

[xiii.] Cipher message 11th March 1944, SAVANNA to Cairo, WO 202/400.

[xiv.] Written account of Eddie Elkington-Smith (date unknown), and recorded account by Charles Keen, 2003.

[xv.] **My Grandad's Story,** Walter Davis and Sharon Black 2007, personal recollections.

[xvi.] www.operationwildhorn.com

Special Note:
Unless otherwise stated, all flight and crew information was sourced from:

148 Operations Record Book, March & April 1944, AIR27/996.

Additional information on operations and Squadron activities from:

148 Operations Record Book Summary, March & April 1944, AIR27/996.

Chapter 5

[i.] **Poland Alone,** Jonathan Walker, The History Press 2008, page 157.

[ii.] Technical information provided by Larry Toft, personal communication, October 2012.

[iii.] **Poland Alone,** Jonathan Walker, The History Press 2008, page 156.

[iv.] **Lotnicze wsparcie Armii Krajowej,** Kajetan Bieniecki, 1994.

[v.] **Poland Alone,** Jonathan Walker, The History Press 2008, page 157.

vi. **Wierchami Karpat,** Jerzy Lyzwa, Instytut Wydawniczy, 1964.

vii. Reconstruction of final moments written with help from Larry Toft, Halifax pilot.

viii. Pamietnik Bronislaw Kaminski (personal diary), courtesy of Pawel Cholewa.

ix. Tom Storey debrief to Brigadier Hill, Moscow, 15th June 1944, CAB 66/53/47, TNA.

x. M.I.9 Debrief, Stradling & Hughes (WO208/3320).

xi. **For Polish Freedom,** A. Nina Mierzwinska-Harper, Partisan Publications 2007.

xii. **My Grandad's Story,** Walter Davis and Sharon Spencer 2007, personal recollection.

xiii. Interview with E. Elkington-Smith conducted by James A. Oliver, 8th February 1996.

Special Note:
Unless otherwise stated, all flight and crew information was sourced from:

148 Operations Record Book, April 1944, AIR27/996.
Bari Flight Log, April 1944, HS4/176.

The sequence of events in this chapter were pieced together using a written account by Eddie Elkington-Smith, a personal recollection by Walter Davis, **My Grandad's Story** co-written by Sharon Spencer in 2007, an account given by Walter Davis to Jonathan Walker for his book, **Poland Alone,** and an account of the Halifax crash by Stanislaw M. Jankowski & Jerzy Piekarczyk, **Ostatni Lot Halifaxa.** Further information came from a personal diary, **Pamietnik Bronislaw Kaminski,** Nina Harper's Book, **For Polish Freedom.** First-hand information from Flight Engineer Charlie Keen in 2003, and lastly, from partisan Bronislaw Smola, interviewed in Tarnogora, April 2013.

Chapter 6

i. **Shot Down & on the Run,** Air Commodore Graham Pitchfork, TNA, page 212.

ii. Information provided by Bronislaw Smola and Piotr Galdys, April 2013.

iii. Conversation with Charlie Keen, 2003.

iv. **Wierchami Karpat,** Jerzy Lyzwa, Instytut Wydawniczy, 1964.

v. **Wierchami Karpat,** Jerzy Lyzwa, Instytut Wydawniczy, 1964.

vi. **Wierchami Karpat,** Jerzy Lyzwa, Instytut Wydawniczy, 1964.

vii. Tom Storey debrief to Brigadier Hill, Moscow, 15 June 1944, CAB 66/53/47, National Archives.

viii. My Grandad's Story, Walter Davis and Sharon Spencer, 2007 personal recollection.

ix. O.W. Congdon, liberated POW interrogation questionnaire, WO344/70.

x. E.E. Smith, liberated POW interrogation questionnaire, WO344/101/1.

xi. Written account by Eddie Elkington-Smith (copy given to Rita Storey).

xii. www.merkki.com A collection of stories, photos, art, and information on Stalag Luft 1.

Special Note:
This chapter has been pieced together using the individual crew debriefs and personal accounts by Eddie Elkington-Smith, Walter Davis, and Charles Keen, plus Jerzy Lyzwa's book, **Wierchami Karpat**, Jankowski & Piekarczyk's book, **Ostatni Lot Halifaxa**, and information from Polish sources during a trip to Poland, April 2013.

Chapter 7

i. Pamietnik "Muchy", Mikolaj Kunicki, Ksiazka i Wiedza, Warszawa 1971.

ii. Pamietnik "Muchy", Mikolaj Kunicki, Ksiazka i Wiedza, Warszawa 1971.

iii. Pamietnik "Muchy", Mikolaj Kunicki, Ksiazka i Wiedza, Warszawa 1971.

iv. Message from Lieutenant General Burrows to Air Commodore Roberts, AIR46/25.

v. Poland Alone, Jonathan Walker, The History Press 2008, page 93.

vi. Translated telegram provided by Paul Lashmar.

vii. Ostatni Lot Halifaxa, Stanislaw Jankowski, Oficyna Cracovia, Krakow 1997.

viii. Personal correspondence to Charles Keen from member of 'Father John's' unit, 1971.

ix. Recorded account by Charles Keen, 2003.

x. Pamietnik "Muchy", Mikolaj Kunicki, Ksiazka i Wiedza, Warszawa 1971.

xi. Tom Storey debrief to Brigadier Hill, Moscow, CAB 66/53/47, National Archives.

xii. Recorded account by Charles Keen, 2003, and Tom Storey's debrief to Brigadier Hill, CAB66/53/47.

xiii. Kunicki letter, Zamosc, 7 March 1958, Stradling family archive.

xiv. Written account by Eddie Elkington-Smith, Storey family archive.

xv. Debrief statement by Walter Davis April 1945.

xvi. Information in this paragraph taken from **My Grandad's Story** by Walter Davis & Sharon Spencer, 2007.

Special Note:
Ostatni Lot Halifaxa by Stanislaw M. Jankowski & Jerzy Piekarczyk has
been a particularly helpful source of information throughout Chapters 5 to 7
and whereas every individual source has not been noted, I could not have
pieced together the sequence of events without this particular book.

Chapter 8

[i.] **Pamietnik "Muchy"**, Mikolaj Kunicki, Ksiazka I Wiedza, Warszawa 1971.
[ii.] Letter to Patrick Stradling from Mikolaj Kunicki, March 1958. Stradling collection.
[iii.] **For Polish Freedom,** A. Nina Mierzwinska-Harper, Partisan Publications 2007, page 128.
[iv.] Message from Air Attaché Moscow Mission to Air Ministry London, 13th June 1944, AIR46/25.
[v.] Message from Lieutenant General Burrows to Air Commodore Roberts, 15th June, 1944, AIR46/25.
[vi.] Message from Air Commodore Roberts of 30 Military Mission to Air Ministry, 18th June, 1944, AIR46/25.
[vii.] Final Report by General Burrows of 30 Military Mission, WO 208/1845.
[viii.] Letter from General Burrows to General Slavin, 15th June 1944, AIR 46/25.
[ix.] **For Polish Freedom,** A. Nina Mierzwinska-Harper, Partisan Publications 2007, page 137.
[x.] **For Polish Freedom,** A. Nina Mierzwinska-Harper, Partisan Publications 2007, page 138.
[xi.] Letter from General Burrows to Mikolaj Kunicki, 15th June 1944, AIR 46/25.
[xii.] Open source on the internet about HMS Matchless
[xiii.] A.M.O. A.1274- A.1311/1942, provided by Mike Hatch, Air Historical Branch 3 (RAF).
[xiv.] IS9 Historical Report, www.arcre.com.
[xv.] **My Grandad's Story,** a personal recollection 2007, Walter Davis & Sharon Spencer.
[xvi.] RAF Escapers, AIR 46/25.
[xvii.] Appendix 11. Locations of British and American Ex-Prisoners of War. 11th March 1945, AIR 46/25.
[xviii.] Personal written recollection, Eddie Elkington-Smith.
[xix.] Letter written by Tom Storey to 'Ali', not dated.

Chapter 9

[i.] TNA WO/373/103, Report on Pte Bloom, 6288542, Alfred James, The Buffs

[ii.] Letter from Jerzy Lyzwa to Pat Stradling, December 12th 1957.

Special Note:

I have pieced this chapter together with the help of letters from the Stradling family archive, generously shared by Mike Bedford Stradling, and letters from the Storey family archive. I have also taken information from **My Grandad's Story**, a personal recollection written by Walter Davis and Sharon Spencer, and from the recollections of Charlie Keen and Eddie Elkington-Smith.

And finally

[i.] **Report on Experience**, John Mulgan, Frontline Books, London 2010, page 121-122.

BIBLIOGRAPHY

Bailey, Roderick, **The Wildest Province,** Vintage Books 2009
Bailey, Roderick, **Forgotten Voices of the Secret War,** Ebury Press 2009.
Bor-Komorowski, **The Secret Army,** The Battery Press 1984.
Conradi, Peter J., **A Very English Hero,** Bloomsbury 2012.
Davidson, Basil, **Partisan Picture,** Bedford Books 1946.
Davis, Walter & Spencer, Sharon, **My Grandad's Story,** unpublished personal document
Davies, Norman, **Rising '44, The Battle for Warsaw**, Pan Books 2004.
Davies, Brigadier 'Trotsky', **Illyrian Venture**, The Bodley Head 1952.
Djilas, Milovan, **Tito, The Story from Inside**, Harcourt Brace Jovanovich 1980.
Gage, Jack, **Greek Adventure**, Unie-Volkspers Beperk, Cape Town 1950.
Hammond, Nicholas, **Venture into Greece**, William Kimber & Co 1983.
Jankowski, Stanislaw Maria & Piekarczyk, Jerzy, **Ostatni Lot Halifaxa**, Oficyna Cracovia 1997.
Jecchinis, Chris, **Beyond Olympus**, George G. Harrap & Co. 1960.
Kunicki, Mikolaj, **Pamietnik Muchy**, Ksiazka I Wiedza, Warsaw 1971.
Lyzwa, Jerzy, **Wierchami Karpat**, Instytut Wydawniczy 1964.
Maclean, Fitzroy, **Eastern Approaches**, Penguin Books, 2009.
Merrick, K.A., **Flights of the Forgotten**, Arms and Armour 1989.
Merrick, K.A., **Halifax From Hell to Victory and Beyond**, Ian Allan Publishing 2009.
Mierzwinska-Harper, A.Nina, **For Polish Freedom**, Partisan Publications 2007.
Mulgan, John, **Report on Experience**, Frontline Books 2010.
Ogden, Alan, **Through Hitler's Back Door**, Pen and Sword, 2010.
Ogden, Alan, **Sons of Odysseus SOE Heroes in Greece**, Bene Factum Publishing 2012.

Ogden, Alan**, A Spur Called Courage SOE Heroes in Italy**, Bene Factum Publishing 2011.

Orpen, Neil, **Airlift to Warsaw, The Rising of 1944**, W. Foulsham & Co. 1984.

Pitchfork, Air Commodore Graham, **Shot Down and on the Run**, TNA 2003.

Porter, Ivor, **Operation Autonomous**, Chatto & Windus 1989.

Porter, Ivor, **Michael of Romania**, Sutton Publishing 2005.

Ritchie, Sebastian, **Our Man in Yugoslavia**, Frank Cass 2004.

Roberts, Walter E., **Tito, Mihailovic and the Allies 1941-1945**, Duke University Press 1987.

Slessor, Sir John, **The Central Blue**, Cassell and Company, 1956.

Stafford, David, **Mission Accomplished SOE and Italy 1943-1945**, Bodley Head 2011.

Stevens, J.M, Woodhouse, C.M & Wallace, D.J., **British Reports on Greece 1943-44**, MTP 1982.

Tilman, H. W., **When Men & Mountains Meet**, Cambridge University Press 1946.

Tudor, Malcolm, **SOE in Italy 1940-1945**, Emilia Publishing 2011.

Walker, Jonathan, **Poland Alone**, The History Press 2008.

Wilkinson, Peter, **Foreign Fields**, I.B. Tauris 1997.

Williams, Heather, **Parachutes, Patriots and Partisans**, Hurst & Company 2003.